Understanding
Your
Teenager

Understanding Your Teenager

Wayne Rice
and
David Veerman

WORD PUBLISHING

NASHVILLE

A Thomas Nelson Company

Published by Word Publishing
Nashville, TN

Drawings by Dan Pegoda

Library of Congress Cataloging-in-Publication Data

Veerman, David.
   Understanding your teenager / by David Veerman, Wayne Rice.
   p. cm.
   ISBN 0-8499-3750-7 (tp)
   1. Teenagers—United States. 2. Adolescence—United States. 3. Parent and teenager—United States. 4. Parenting—United States. I. Rice, Wayne. II. Title.
   HQ796.V423 1999
   305.235—dc21
                                             99-30289
                                               CIP

Printed in the United States of America
99 00 01 02 03 04 05 06 BVG 9 8 7 6 5 4 3 2 1

Contents

Introduction

"Congratulations! It's a teenager!" Consider the chaos if a delivery room doctor were to make such an announcement to new parents. "Wait a minute! That's not right—there must be some mistake," Mom and Dad would shout. That's because the usual course of child rearing begins with the birth of a tiny baby, not an adolescent.

Surely a birth is a blessed event, but even a baby takes some getting used to. Then that life stage is followed quickly by infant, toddler, and young child. Most parents assume, therefore, that by the time the teenage years roll around, they will have gotten the hang of this parenting gig.

Not so fast, pubescent breath! The shocking truth is that the arrival of every teenager in a home seems abrupt, sudden, as though a new person has just been dumped unceremoniously into the family—as shocking as the doctor's surprise announcement above. And even more disturbing is the realization that all previous parenting experiences suddenly seem irrelevant. What Mom and Dad did with the children when they were younger seems to have no bearing on the teenage years.

This insight sneaks up on most parents. One day Dad is wrestling and tickling on the floor with his little boy; the next day the boy is defiantly demanding that he be allowed to have his tongue pierced. One day Mom is amazed at her little girl's cute precociousness as she strings together her first sentence and then, a year or so later, as she regales everyone with minute-by-minute accounts of her day. But now the daughter's language consists of grunts, sighs, and rolled eyes. Just yesterday the parents were holding precious, helpless babies in their arms. Today, the kids can take them, two out of three falls.

It happened so fast, so suddenly, and parents wonder: *How? Why?* and *Now what do we do?*

That's why we wrote *Understanding Your Teenager*. As the title implies, the purpose of this book is to help you better understand what's going on in the life of your adolescent son or daughter. We believe that understanding kids leads to a better relationship with them, strengthens our faith in them, and provides us with hope for the future. We want you to be able to enjoy your children during their teen years as much (or more!) as you did when they were little.

There's more here than just information, however. It's not enough for parents to simply *understand* teenagers. We must act on what we know—put it into practice. So we've included lots of practical help and ideas, proven ways for responding appropriately based on what we know about adolescent development and good parenting.

We also want to encourage you and affirm you in your role as the parent of a teenager. Don't let anyone convince you that you no longer matter when your kids become adolescents. One thing we have learned from years of working with other people's kids in various youth ministries is that parents remain the most important people in the lives of teenagers—all the way through their high school years. Kids who thrive during their adolescence usually have parents who care enough to understand them and stay involved. Your efforts to be a better parent will pay off.

We have tried not to approach this topic as "experts" (we used to be experts until our own kids entered adolescence). We are not psychologists or family therapists. Rather, we are two people who have been there—parents who have experienced what you are now experiencing. As youth workers, we have had the opportunity to observe and interact with thousands of teenagers over the years—but more important, we have struggled with all of the issues in our own families, with our own teens. We've survived—and, so far, so have our kids. So please accept what we write as help from a couple of friends who can empathize and understand what you are going through.

We divided the book into two parts. The first focuses on the characteristics of teenagers today and their changing world. Our goal here is to help you gain a greater appreciation for what's going on in the life of your teen. Adolescence is an awesome and sacred time of life—it is not a disease to be cured. We hope that as you read through this material, you will gain new respect for the process that every young person goes through on his or her journey to adulthood. We have a very positive view of adolescence, despite the fact that it is filled with challenges, both for teens and parents.

The second part shifts to principles of effective parenting. This is our short list of things to remember when your children become teenagers. We hope that you will see this as a sort of road map for parenting teens—it's easy to feel lost these days. These principles will help you stay on the right track and give you practical suggestions for what to do and where to go. Please see them as guidelines, not guarantees or formulas.

The concepts and ideas in this book are presented at dozens of Understanding Your Teenager seminars held in cities and communities across North America every year. (For more information on these seminars, see page 287) We want to thank current and past members of the UYT seminar team for their contributions to this material—especially Stan Beard, Dr. Bill

Rowley, and David Lynn, who were part of the original design team. We would also like to thank Kendra Smiley for her generous contribution of material to this book.

Well, that's about all the introductory stuff we can think of, except to say: Thanks for buying this book and for being a parent who cares about his or her kids. That alone says a lot about your chances for success!

Part I

The Changing World
of Today's Teen

Chapter 1

Teens Are Growing up in a Different World

W hat? What do you mean I can't go?!" Kyle almost screamed as he slammed his books on the kitchen table.

"Your father and I talked it over," Marge Thompson spoke slowly and calmly, ignoring Kyle's outburst and trying to control her own temper, "and we don't think that's the kind of music you should be listening to. We've heard about that group—their life styles and the things they promote. They're just not . . ."

"You must be kidding," Kyle interrupted. "Everyone knows it's just a show, and besides, all my friends are going, even kids from church! You are so strict—I can't do anything! Look, Mom, it's different now. You just don't understand."

"Now wait just a minute, young man—" Becoming agitated, Marge began to raise her voice. "We may have rules and standards, but we're not that strict. Not so long ago, I was a teenager. In fact, when I was your age . . ."

Does any of that dialogue sound familiar? You may have heard a speech like Kyle's, or perhaps you felt the tension along with Marge. But even if a similar scene has never played in your house, you probably recognize at least one line—*When I was your age . . .* That must be the most often repeated phrase used by parents worldwide. And it's one of those statements that we swore we would never say after hearing it countless times in our own growing-up years. Yet the words spill out—we've become our parents!

"When I was your age . . ." Flip back over those years to when you were a teenager. What pressures and problems did you face between twelve and twenty? When did you learn about sex, and how did you deal with sexual temptation? What kind of a driver were you? Were you part of the "in crowd"? If you are like most adults, you can remember some pretty rough moments during junior and senior high. Peer pressure and temptation were real, and you remember doing things you shouldn't have, without your parents' knowledge. Hmm, maybe that's why you have trouble trusting your kids today.

In about 500 B.C., Socrates described teenagers this way: "Youth today love luxury. They have bad manners, contempt for authority, no respect for older people, and talk nonsense when they should work. Young people do not stand up any longer when adults enter the room. They contradict their parents, talk too much in company, guzzle their food, lay their legs on the table, and tyrannize their elders."[1]

With a few minor changes, that could describe teens today. This is nothing new. And today's kids are a lot like we were at that age. Teenagers have been driving adults crazy for a long time, all the while asking the same fundamental questions: Who am I? What am I going to be? Does anybody like me? Am I OK? —questions of identity, purpose, and meaning.

The Good Old Days?

I see no hope for the future of our people if they are dependent upon the frivolous youth of today, for certainly all youth are reckless beyond words. When I was a boy, we were taught to be discreet and respectful of elders, but the present youth are exceedingly wild and impatient of restraint.

—Hestes, the Greek poet, circa 800 B.C.

The world is passing through troubled times. The young people of today think of nothing but themselves. They have no reverence for parents or old age; they talk as if they knew everything and what passes for wisdom with us is foolishness for them.

—Peter the Herman, who spearheaded the first crusade, circa A.D. 1274

This is helpful to remember because the best way to begin to understand teenagers is not to learn how different kids are today but to have a good memory. If we can remember our own adolescence, we will be able to understand much of what our kids are experiencing.

So if kids haven't changed that much and our own experience *can* give us insight into our kids, then it's all right to say, "When I was your age . . ." Right?

Probably not. Because the *context* of adolescence has changed. Although just a couple of decades have passed since our teenage years, in a very real sense, life is different these days . . . mainly because the world has changed dramatically.

IT'S A DIFFERENT WORLD

Whether you were a teenager during the 1960s, 1970s, or 1980s, times have changed. Here are a few of the ways that things are different now.

Loss of Support

Kids today don't have the kind of natural built-in support systems they had in the past, mainly because the extended family is extinct. In the past, children and youth were surrounded by a network of family members who lived in the same geographical area. A kid could access adult relatives at almost any time, and for free. These people had a vested interest in how the young person turned out, and they provided love and encouragement. For example, according to the 1940 census, 70 percent of all households in America had at least one grandparent living in the home. Today, for a variety of reasons, that figure has dropped to just 2 percent. In effect, this is the first generation in history to completely reverse its way of raising children.

For literally thousands of years, children were raised in the context of extended families, not nuclear families. The idealized nuclear family of 1950s television (*Leave It to Beaver, Ozzie and Harriet,* and so forth) is, in reality, a twentieth-century phenomenon that resulted when families moved away from the farm and into the suburbs. Prior to World War II, parents were not expected to raise children alone. They had lots of help.

Scattered

I was born in Chicago and reared in Rockford. I went to college in Wheaton and to graduate school in Deerfield. Then I worked for ten years in Park Ridge and DesPlaines—*all in Illinois*. My parents, brothers, and sister lived nearby, so it was convenient to spend holidays and special occasions with the family. My wife's parents and brother lived in the Detroit area—a little farther away, but only five hours.

Then suddenly, in the space of about one year, one brother moved to Washington, D.C., another brother moved to Connecticut, and we moved to Louisiana. Then another brother went to college in Minnesota. Suddenly my family was scattered.

And we haven't lived close together since.

—Dave Veerman

If 1940 seems too long ago, consider your own family and your growing-up years. Just twenty or thirty years ago, most Americans expected to live in the same area most of their lives, with the breadwinner of the family employed by one employer during most of that time. The great exceptions were military families who seemed to move every year or two. But in general, children born in the Midwest tended to stay in the Midwest, those born in the East tended to stay in the East, and so forth; these children lived fairly close to grandparents, aunts, uncles, and other relatives.

Today, however, the opposite is true—those who live their whole lives in one community are the exceptions. Whether the moves are required by a corporation or by new jobs and opportunities, today's Americans are increasingly mobile. Interview the family who just moved in next door or the young couple who just started attending your church, and you'll probably learn that they have already moved several times and now live far away from parents and siblings. Maybe all you have to do is reflect on your own experience—how often have you moved in the past decade?

As a result of this family scattering, children, especially teenagers, have lost their natural support systems—grandparents and other relatives who, in the past, served as mentors and buffers against parents who overdisciplined or made mistakes. Teenagers don't have cousins, aunts, uncles, and grandparents close by to offer counsel and comfort and to help point the way. When you were young, you probably stayed out of trouble because you would have disappointed too many people, and you wanted to make those people proud of you. Many of today's teenagers have no one like that. Nobody really cares what they do.

Mothers and fathers also lose in this system. They no longer receive coaching from their parents and other relatives on how to parent their children. And just as their kids hit adolescence, many must also deal with the problems of aging parents, exacerbated by the distance that separates them from Mom and Dad. This can add tremendous stress to families.

In addition to the loss of the extended family, there has been a similar and corresponding loss of community. Most people today know the characters on their favorite TV sitcom better than they know their next-door neighbors. In the past, you could count on neighbors and friends in the community to help you parent your children. Today, the common wisdom is to stay out of other people's business. We have become a nation of isolated individuals who are afraid to get involved in the affairs of our neighbors and friends. So we leave each other alone.

With the loss of the extended family and the loss of community, our children experience a new kind of aloneness in today's world, especially when even their parents are absent. Because of this, some have characterized today's kids as suffering from "relational deprivation." Patricia Hersch, in *A Tribe Apart*, notes that today's teenagers spend only 4.8 percent of their time with their parents and only 2 percent of their time with adults who are not their parents.[2] This is a huge change in how children

All Alone

The most stunning change for adolescents today is their aloneness. The adolescents of the nineties are more isolated and more unsupervised than other generations. It used to be that kids sneaked time away from adults. The proverbial kisses stolen in the backseat of a car, or the forbidden cigarette smoked behind the garage, bestowed a grown-up thrill of getting away with the forbidden. The real excitement was in not getting caught by a watchful (or nosy) neighbor who'd call Mom. Today Mom is at work. Neighbors are often strangers. Relatives live in distant places. This changes everything. It changes access to a bed, a liquor cabinet, a car. The kids have all the responsibility for making decisions, often in a void, or they create an ersatz family with their buddies and let them decide. These days youngsters can easily do more good or bad without other people knowing about it.

Patricia Hersch, *A Tribe Apart* (New York: Fawcett-Columbine, 1998), 19–20.

are raised. William Mahedy and Janet Bernardi have noted in *A Generation Alone* that today's youth have been abandoned by their parents, their families, their cultures, their institutions, and their world—and it is this abandonment that has become the root cause for practically every disorder that we see in today's kids.[3]

Today's teenagers and their parents have lost their support. And with this loss of support, it's a different world.

Loss of Place

In the distant past, in an agrarian society, a new child meant another worker, eventually, for the family farm. As society moved away from the country, children still were seen as potential workers because, in communities of every size, they were needed to take over family businesses. Even decades later, with the rise of corporate America, kids still were needed to do family chores—they contributed to the family economy and were viewed as assets. Parents looked forward to the day when their children could take on responsibility and help support the family.

These days, however, rather than being assets, children, especially adolescents, are viewed as liabilities or luxuries. As a result, this is the first generation of young people in history to be totally unnecessary. Every year at least one major publication will have a feature article on how much it costs to raise a child from birth through college. "It's expensive," blare the headlines, and kids get the message (especially when parents remind them of how much they cost). Imagine what this does to the self-image of teenagers. They feel no inherent importance or self-worth. As a result, they are very vulnerable to exploitation and problem behavior.

Edward A. Wynne and Thomas Einstein of the University of

Chicago wrote this about today's kids: "The most typical characteristic of adolescents today is that no one really needs them. And they know it. . . . This does not mean that most adolescents are not loved or enjoyed. But their roles are largely ornamental. If most of them died, the immediate day-to-day work of the world would continue."[4]

The Cost of Children

Of course they're cute. But have you any idea how much one will set you back? A hardheaded inquiry.

Let's face it: Children don't come free. Indeed, their cost is rising. According to one government calculation, the direct cost of raising a child to age eighteen has risen by 20 percent since 1960 (adjusted for inflation and changes in family size). And this calculation doesn't take into account the forgone wages that result from a parent taking time off to raise children—an economic cost that has skyrocketed during the last generation as women have entered the work force in unprecedented numbers. . . .

What we've found is that the typical child in a middle-income family requires a twenty-two-year investment of just over $1.45 million. That's a pretty steep price tag in a country where the median income for families with children is just $41,000. The child's unit cost rises to $2.78 million for the top-third income bracket and drops to $761,871 for the bottom-third income bracket.

Phillip J. Longman, "The Cost of Children," *U.S. News & World Report* (30 March 1998), 51–54.

Indeed, if teenagers disappeared, the only disruption to the day-to-day work of the world would be in those areas where youth are needed as consumers. The entertainment, fast-food, clothing, and sneaker industries would likely be disrupted by the disappearance of adolescents, but little else.

In addition, today's kids have less physical space allotted to them in which to grow up. In rural cultures, children had acres of land to use as a playground or a place to explore. Even in the city, neighborhoods and parks were safe havens for youth in need of space to run and play. But land is no longer available, and the safety of the neighborhood is gone.

"Fifty years ago it was possible to tell children to go out and play, even in urban areas," David Elkind remembers. "But today, many urban and suburban communities are no longer safe for children."[5] In recent years, youth have turned to the shopping malls of America for a place to hang out, but even those are now becoming off-limits for kids. Some of the largest shopping malls have pulled up the welcome mat for teenagers and now require them to be accompanied by an adult.

Teenagers have lost their place. And with this loss of place, it's a different world.

Loss of Innocence

We live in what is called the "information age." Simply put, this just means that more people know more about the world than ever before. Modern technology has begotten personal computers, cell phones, fax machines, E-mail, and the Internet. Today we communicate with people worldwide almost instantly. Even wars are televised. And consider the proliferation of news programs. In addition to the CNN channels, each of the major networks features several "news magazines" as well as prime-time news broadcasts.

At the same time, much of popular media have been going to the limits and beyond in their programs, becoming increasingly explicit and extreme in language, violence, sex talk and acts, and "adult" themes. As a result of this media and information blitz, today's kids are exposed to so much more. Even elementary students know about drugs, suicide, kidnappings, and presidential affairs. When the transcripts of Monica Lewinsky's testimony hit the Internet, concerned parents wondered how to handle the barrage of questions from their children about the salacious activities in the Oval Office.

In *The Disappearance of Childhood*, Neil Postman argues that childhood and adolescence once was a time when kids were protected and shielded from certain kinds of information. Young people were given a safe and stress-free environment in which to grow and develop, where they didn't have to deal with the kinds of pressures that adults face. But today, even very young children are exposed to every sort of human depravity and vice under the mistaken assumption that bad experiences will somehow better prepare them for adulthood. In reality, the reverse is true. A good experience is the best preparation for a bad one. Regular exposure to disturbing information only traumatizes children and creates stress that interferes with their progress. Today's kids have simply seen too much, experienced too much, and done too much. That's why today's kids are sometimes called the "Been There, Done That" generation.

This loss of innocence means that kids don't have the chance to just be kids, free from the worries of the adult world. No wonder they are the newest victims of stress in our society.

Teenagers have lost their innocence. And with this loss of innocence, it's a different world.

Loss of Absolutes

In his best-selling and eyeopening book *Future Shock*, Alvin Toffler discussed "information overload" and "decision stress." And that was in 1970! Toffler's thesis was that with so much technological and communication advancement, we were becoming inundated with choices, often leading to a sort of choice stress. For many, the situation was comparable to a person from a Third World country walking the aisles of an American grocery store. In the home country, *if* there was a store, the person might find one brand of breakfast cereal on the shelves. But in the American supermarket, our visitor would be confronted with a seemingly endless number and variety of brands and sizes—a tremendous difference and a great culture shock.

Toffler's book has proved to be very insightful and prophetic, for today we have scores of options in every area of life. For example, with a satellite dish and a handy remote, we now can choose from among hundreds of television stations, and the Internet features millions of home pages. This generation is bombarded with choices.

The vast array of choices moves well beyond products and services. Religions, life styles, and values also come in a wide variety of shapes and sizes. That's why pundits often intone that we live in a "pluralistic society"—a smorgasbord of philosophies, theologies, and ideologies compete for allegiance.

Here's how the information age plays out with parents and teens:

World of the Parent	World of the Teenager
Knew about wars through newspaper and TV news	Watches wars on TV

Read about Muslims, Hindus, and Buddhists	Has Muslim, Hindu, and Buddhist friends
Heard about drugs in far-off cities	Knows where to get almost any kind of drug
Pornography limited to X-rated venues	Hard-core pornography a mouse click away
Knew only the public image of celebrities	Knows the "secret" lives of celebrities
Was taught homosexuality was deviant behavior	Is taught being gay is an alternative life style

You could probably add to this chart. What a contrast between the two worlds! As John Naisbett observed more than twenty years ago in his book, *Megatrends*, our society is rapidly moving from an either-or society to a multiple-choice society.

With this recurring theme of pluralism comes the strong message that we must be tolerant of others, regardless of their beliefs or life style. In fact, the only thing that isn't tolerated is intolerance. There are no absolutes, and everything is OK, we are told; it's just a matter of personal preference and choice.

A generation or two ago, there was something like a national consensus of values. What was taught in the home and the church was generally affirmed or at least left unquestioned by the media, the school, and the government. Today, that kind of support for traditional family (or Judeo-Christian) values no longer exists, and more often than not those values are directly challenged by the institutions that used to support them. One national television network recently advertised its fall lineup of programming with this slogan: "Guaranteed to break at least 20 percent more commandments than any other lineup!"[6]

With this loss of absolutes comes a loss of boundaries and

the sense of right and wrong, good and bad, true and false. Kids, especially teenagers who are trying to make their own decisions and choose their own values, can feel overwhelmed by all the options available to them. Many get stuck and avoid making decisions at all, fearing they will make the wrong one.

With this loss of absolutes, it's a different world.

Loss of Heroes

It probably began in the 1960s and 1970s when our generation rebelled against authority. Certainly it was accelerated by the explosion of investigative reporting in the wake of Water-gate. A definite contributing factor has to be the proliferation of information media. Then add to the mix the breakdown of the family. Whatever the reason or combination of causes, our kids have grown up not trusting their government, their parents, their leaders, their teachers, their heroes, and, most of all, their institutions. Too many cultural icons have been smashed; too many bronze statues have been discovered to have feet of clay; too many adults have disappointed.

The distrust is universal: No occupation or walk of life is immune. Sports stars, religious gurus, professors, and presidents have fallen. And every day promises a scandalous revelation about yet another national figure.

As a result, teenagers have few, if any, authentic heroes, role models to whom they can look for positive examples. When asked, "Whom do you admire?" the number one response was, "No one."

With this loss of heroes, it's a different world.

Many other changes have taken place in society, of course, and it's helpful to remember that not all of the changes are negative. Advances in medicine, education, communication, transportation, world peace, environmental safety, and economics have made positive contributions to our overall quality of life. But as Alvin Toffler wrote, "Change itself is changing."[7] Changes take place much more rapidly than they did a generation or two ago, and sometimes it's easy to become overwhelmed by all of them.

With all these differences and changes in the world, what can we do? How should we respond?

WHAT TO DO

Try to empathize. We should try to remember our own adolescent years.

All Alone

How Well Do You Remember?

Think back to your teenage years for a moment:
- What did you do for fun?
- What were the biggest fads when you were in high school?
- What secrets did you keep from your parents?
- What was your biggest problem?
- Who were your best friends?
- Who were some of the most popular entertainers and sports heroes?
- What arguments did you have with your parents?
- What did you do well?

Do you remember what it was like to be a teenager? Now put yourself in today's world. What kind of a person do you think you would be? What kinds of TV shows do you think you would watch? In what activities would you participate? How would you spend your spare time? Questions like these will help you to understand why your teenager acts the way he or she does.

Try to keep a positive attitude. It's often difficult for older people to appreciate change or to see any value in new things. Many older people still refuse to even consider buying a computer, cell phone, or CD player (so what's wrong with my record player?) because they just don't see any good in any of them. We need to try to avoid getting prematurely old by refusing to accept anything that feels like change.

Avoid blaming kids for things over which they have no control. It's not their fault that the world is different; it's not their fault that there is no place for them or heroes to admire. Sometimes we blame kids inadvertently by getting all over them for the clothes they wear, the music they listen to, the TV shows they watch, and the activities they participate in. But they didn't create all of the options and the compelling advertisements. This is the world they have been given. The chances are pretty good that if we were their age, we'd be wearing the same silly clothes and listening to those bands with strange names too.

Avoid idealizing the past. We live in the present, and we really couldn't turn back the clock to those good old days of yesteryear, even if we wanted to. In reality, the good old days weren't nearly as wonderful as we remember them. The reason that the phrase "When I was your age" just doesn't have much meaning to kids is that we never were their age. We never had to grow up in a world quite like the one our kids are growing up in. So when your teenager rolls his or her eyes and says, "But it's not the same!" believe it.

That Was Then; This Is Now

Then, most children grew up in two-parent families. *Now*, less than half do.

Then, only one parent had to work outside the home. *Now*, both parents do.

Then, children had extended families living nearby. *Now*, the extended family is extinct.

Then, youth were given jobs on the farm or in the community. *Now*, they have little responsibility at all.

Then, children entertained themselves. *Now*, children are entertained by the media.

Then, there was universal respect for authority. *Now*, children are taught to question authority.

Then, neighborhoods were safe places for children to run and play. *Now*, children are at risk in their own backyards.

Then, there was a national consensus of values and morality. *Now*, values are left up to the individual.

Then, children were protected from information about sex. *Now*, sexual messages are everywhere.

Then, most entertainment was family-friendly. *Now*, most entertainment is "for mature audiences only."

Then, the church played a central role in family and community life. *Now*, the church has been marginalized.

Then, growing up was easy. *Now* . . . ?

Respond appropriately to the changes that have taken place in our teenagers' world. We need to understand that we may have to do some things with our kids that our parents didn't find necessary. For example, in today's world of information overload, we will probably need to talk more with our kids about what they are being exposed to, particularly in the area of sexual morality. Or, given that today's world is faster paced and families are busier than ever before, it could be that we will need to be more intentional about scheduling family time for relationship building with our kids. Or, if our teenagers lack the opportunities we had to feel needed and valued as contributing members of society, we may want to connect them with service organizations or church youth ministries that involve students in leadership-building activities and service projects.

Changes in modern society don't have to cause panic, frustration, or retreat. Instead, these changes can provide us with an opportunity to be creative and involved with our kids in new ways. The Chinese symbol for the word *crisis* means both opportunity and danger. Yes, there are dangers inherent in many of the changes that impact our families, but there are also opportunities to demonstrate the power and influence of parents who love enough to act.

It's a different world!

THINK IT THROUGH

1. When you were between the ages of twelve and twenty, in what ways were you similar to your children?
2. When you were a teenager, what extended family members (grandparents, aunts, uncles, cousins) lived within an hour's drive?

3. How close do you live to your parents today? When did you move away?

4. What relative do you wish you could see more often?

5. What would be the ideal distance between you and your grown children?

6. When did (do) you feel most stretched financially by your children?

7. In what ways do your teenagers contribute to the family?

8. What can you do to help your kids feel more wanted and needed?

9. When you were in high school, how many channels could you get on the family TV? How many do you have now?

10. How many phones does your family own? In what ways has modern technology improved communication within the family? In what ways has it made communication worse?

11. Which of the following do you have for your home? satellite dish ___, video games ___, Internet access ___, caller ID ___, cellular phone ___, fax machine ___. Which do you wish you didn't have? Why?

12. What were the most difficult choices that you had to make as a teenager?

13. Who were your heroes? Who are the adult role models for your teenagers?

14. When are you most tempted to say, "When I was your age . . ."?

Teens Are in Transition

Hey, needle nose!" the tall boy yelled across the playground. "Whatcha been smellin' lately?" He laughed along with the boys surrounding him.

Jamie wanted to yell back, but he thought better of it and just continued walking toward school, pretending not to hear. Of course he *had* heard, just as he'd heard a dozen other similar comments and taunts during this year. He hated the way he looked, especially his face and the nose that seemed to dominate it. He sure didn't remember having such a big nose. *When did* that *happen?* he wondered.

Think back again to your adolescent years. When was your awkward stage? When did you have your growth spurt? Some kids grow early and others, late (and, as Jamie discovered, usually the nose, feet, and hands grow first). In either case, the growth that happens during the preteen and teenage years can be frustrating, confusing, and painful. And these growth spurts occur in *every area* of life as teenagers move from childhood to adulthood.

Yes, our teens are in transition, the biggest transition in life. They aren't just growing faster at adolescence, they are also quite literally changing, experiencing a metamorphosis similar to a butterfly emerging from a chrysalis. Children cease to be children as their eyes are opened to a whole new world of adulthood. At puberty, they get not only a new body but a new brain and a new understanding of the world and their place in it as well. Puberty changes everything. H. Stephen Glenn defines *puberty* as "when massive doses of progesterone and testosterone come roaring into the body, setting off a biophysical disaster of unprecedented proportions."[1]

One of the biggest changes is psychological. A new and powerful voice rises up inside of children, telling them that they are no longer little boys or little girls. "It's time to be independent—to take control of your own life!" Children feel compelled to obey this voice that sets them on a collision course with their parents. Because childhood is marked by domination by parents, it follows that adolescents must turn away from their parents. Thus begins the quest for autonomy, which we will discuss in chapter 3.

We should not minimize these changes or underestimate the significance of this dramatic time of transition.

RITES OF PASSAGE?

In the past in our culture and even today in many other cultures, a rite of passage celebrated and confirmed a child's entrance into adulthood. Native American tribes, for example, conducted a ceremony for the occasion of a girl's first menstruation. This was a physical sign that the girl had become a young woman and was ready to be accepted into the adult community. Native American boys were given similar rites of passage, even though they didn't have such a clear physical indicator of their emerging manhood. At a certain age, they were taken off in the company of the men, tutored in the duties and privileges of being an adult, and allowed to emerge officially as a man. Among some Native American tribes, a boy went out alone on a "vision quest" and returned, reborn, with a new name—his name as a man.

Such rites of passage seem almost prehistoric today, but they served an important function for societies of the past. Children tended to adjust better to adulthood when they had a clear understanding of where they stood and what others thought of them.

These days, parents have few rites of passage for their children. Instead, we ask our young adolescents to wait another eight or ten years (nearly double their age at the time) before they can assume the mantle of adulthood. Some youth don't think of themselves as adults even after they enter their twenties.

Perhaps the only rite of passage for the average teenager today is obtaining a driver's license. For most teens, getting this license is a highly significant event that symbolizes their acceptance into the adult world.

ADOLESCENT OR YOUNG ADULT?

Today it is much more difficult for children to make a smooth transition into adulthood because of what has been called "the invention of adolescence." Early in the twentieth century, psychologists began writing about adolescence as a unique and separate stage of life—between childhood and adulthood—and this changed forever how people think about human development.

No longer do children become adults when they reach puberty. Now, they become *adolescents*. This is a relatively new way of thinking. In the past, we regarded youngsters who were twelve or thirteen years old as young adults, or "young

Teenagers

The label "teenager" first appeared commonly in American culture about 1955. That's why we know so little about them—they were invented in 1955. Always before we had dealt with "children" and "young people" and knew what to do with each. Only when millions of "baby boomers" entered adolescence with no meaningful role to play and without the support of extended family . . . in a world where parents had planned to support them through four years of college . . . did we begin to experience the universal "craziness" that we see today in young people assigned to limbo during this critical developmental stage. So we labeled them "teenagers." If we think about it, this is a stereotype which says the most significant thing about a young person between 13 and 19 years of age is the "1" in front of their age.

H. Stephen Glenn in *Positive Discipline for Teenagers*, by Jane Nelson and Lynn Lott (Rocklin, CA: Prima Publishing, 1994), foreword.

people," but today we call them *teenagers* or *early* adolescents (not quite an adolescent). Interestingly, the word *teenager* was also invented in the twentieth century. It didn't appear in American dictionaries until the 1950s.

The invention of adolescence, by the way, is what led to the development of "youth culture" as we know it today—the world of the junior and senior high school, with its own language, music, dress, economy, and customs, completely separate and different from the world of adults. This was not the case prior to modern times. For thousands of years, there were only two stages of life: childhood and adulthood. You were either a child or you were an adult. At puberty, you changed from one to the other.

That's one reason why it is so hard to find any mention of adolescence in the Bible. Adolescence didn't exist in Bible times. The word *youth*, when it does appear, is more accurately translated "young person" or "young adult." Paul wrote, "When I was a child, I talked like a child, I thought like a child, I reasoned like a child. When I became a man, I put childish ways behind me" (1 Cor. 13:11). This begs the question "When did Paul become a man?" Today, we might estimate his age at eighteen, or perhaps twenty-one. But Paul was most likely referring to his bar mitzvah, which occurred, as it did for most Jewish boys, around the age of twelve. The purpose of a bar mitzvah, then as now, is to inaugurate a young man's entry into adulthood, to celebrate his new status and position in the community.

In today's world, however, children don't become adults when they reach adolescence; they become teenagers. This poses a problem for both children and parents because no one really knows what a teenager is supposed to be. By default, teens themselves have created their own world apart from adults, and adults have chosen to just leave them alone. The long-term negative impact of the invention of adolescence has been the almost total isolation of adolescents from the people who can teach them the most—adults.

Public Recognition

Confirmation, bar or bas mitzvah, graduation exercises, and the like provide a public acknowledgment that young people have attained new levels of maturity. Public recognition confirms teenagers in their sense of progress and growth.

David Elkind, *All Grown Up and No Place to Go* (Reading, MA: Addison-Wesley, 1984), 93.

In the past, adults considered adolescents to be a lot like themselves, only younger. Adolescents were welcome around adults. That's not the case today. Many adults are afraid of teenagers and feel uncomfortable around them. As a result, teens don't get the kind of mentoring and encouragement that they need to become confident and capable in their adulthood. It takes a lot longer today for kids to grow up.

This diagram illustrates the transition from childhood to adulthood:

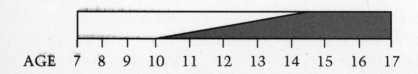

AGE 7 8 9 10 11 12 13 14 15 16 17

When children reach adolescence at around age ten or eleven, they begin the process of changing from a child to an adult. With each passing day, they become more of an adult and less of a child. The transformation is usually complete by age fifteen or sixteen. Teenagers still have plenty of maturing to do, but at this point they have the physical and intellectual tools to do so. When teens are treated more like adults and less like children, their maturing comes sooner rather than later.

Because all these changes occur during these short years, teenagers come in all shapes, sizes, and stages of maturity. Adolescence is the time in between—a time of change, of transition.

EVERY AREA OF LIFE!

Not only are the changes dramatic, but they also appear in every area of life.

Physical

The physical changes are the most obvious. We can see them as adolescents grow like crazy and seem to metamorphose overnight. These changes can be traumatic for both parents and teens.

> Our son's biggest rite of passage: the day he answered the phone and was *not* asked if he was his mom.
>
> —Kendra Smiley

Consider the typical eighth-grade girl. Because girls tend to mature sooner than boys, she probably towers over the boys in her school. She may only be 5'9", but in a school of 5-foot boys, she feels like a giant. She may even begin to stoop her shoulders in an unconscious effort to shrink an inch or two.

Physical Changes During Adolescence

For both boys and girls
- Increased height and weight
- Growth of pubic hair
- Increased activity of sweat glands
- Growth of armpit hair
- Deepening of voice (more for boys than for girls)
- Growth of hair on face and body (more for boys than for girls)
- Possible complexion problems (acne)
- Growth of fat-bearing cells

For girls only
- Development of ovaries and uterus
- First period (menstruation or *menarche*)
- Development of breasts
- Widening of hips

For boys only
- Development of penis and testicles
- Involuntary ejaculation (wet dreams)
- Enlargement of neck
- Broadening of shoulders
- Growth of muscle tissue

Many eighth- and ninth-grade girls look much older than their age, with shapely figures. And with hormones coursing through their bodies, they may be confused about their sexual feelings and become boy crazy. One father described his daughter as having a sixteen-year-old physical plant run by a twelve-year-old "board of directors." Unfortunately, many of these girls fall prey to older boys who like what they see and ask them out (often with dubious motives).

While some junior high boys have put on height and weight, many still look like little kids. The bigger and stronger boys are often tabbed as the featured players on the football and basketball teams, while the smaller ones ride the bench. The smaller boys feel like shrimps next to these bigger boys and the girls.

And then there's the issue of coordination. Because the feet grow first, rapidly growing early adolescents tend to be uncoordinated, often tripping when they run or just walk up the stairs. Check out the boys in a church junior high youth group, and you'll probably find a few wearing size 13 or larger shoes. Eventually the rest of their bodies will catch up, but right now they're nowhere near six feet tall. Some boys don't begin to grow until their junior or senior year in high school.

Early adolescent bodies change dramatically when everyone else's doesn't—or don't change when everyone else's does. Either case can be quite traumatic! Look at any group of twelve-year-olds and you will see up to six years of difference between their minds and their bodies (in either direction).

Puberty brings a host of frustrations, including acne, an increasing interest in the opposite sex, and seemingly uncontrollable sexual urges. These physical changes can be very confusing and can lead to a variety of unusual behaviors. For example, early adolescents will do strange things to get the attention of a member of the opposite sex, tell dirty jokes, and use explicit language (this also makes them feel older), and they may experiment with sex. Usually this is when boys begin masturbating, and they can become enamored with pornography. This mix of feelings, thoughts, and, sometimes, actions can result in tremendous guilt, especially for young people from strong Christian backgrounds.

These rapid physical changes can lead to a myriad of problems, not the least of which is a negative self-concept. As we saw at the beginning of the chapter, kids this age can be quite cruel toward each other. Think back—which of your physical features drew ridicule? When did you make a fool of yourself with the opposite sex? Most adults have painful memories of the growing years and can recall specific humiliating experiences. In fact, we may even carry those negative nicknames in the back of our minds, allowing them to affect how we see ourselves today.

Teenagers are changing physically.

Intellectual

Another area where teenagers experience tremendous growth is in their ability to think and reason. Early adolescents are moving from "concrete operations" to "formal operations." In other words, they switch from thinking concretely to thinking conceptually. Later, usually in college, they will learn to think analytically.

We can see the differences between concrete and conceptual thinking in the types of jokes kids appreciate. Young children laugh at people and animals that look and sound silly. The actions are concrete; that is, they can be seen and understood. Adults, on the other hand, appreciate jokes with subtle punch lines that take them by surprise—a play on words, a misunderstanding, a humorous situation, and so forth. In the middle, some teenagers will consider slapstick humor to be "stupid" (interpreted, "too young"), while others "don't get" the more sophisticated jokes.

Or consider the differences in Sunday school. Younger children eagerly learn the exciting Bible stories such as Adam and Eve, Jonah and the Great Fish, and David and Goliath as their teachers teach with crafts and object lessons. At the other end of the educational spectrum, adults discuss deep theological concepts such as Christ's substitutionary atonement and the lordship of Christ. Adolescents, in the middle of these two extremes, both in their ability to learn and in the content taught, struggle to put the Bible stories into historical context and wonder aloud how God makes sense in their lives *today*.

Good teachers understand and appreciate these differences. Therefore, a teacher of third graders will use objects to illustrate a point and will get students involved in hands-on learning experiences. College professors, however, may lecture for an hour while students take notes and think about the concepts and lessons being taught.

For teenagers, especially early adolescents who are making the transition from concrete to conceptual thinking, school can be an exhilarating adventure or a discouraging experience as they are presented with an array of facts and concepts. During these years, some students may jump ahead, discovering the world of ideas, opening their imaginations, and understanding the potential results of their choices and actions. But others may be left behind, ignored by teachers who gravitate toward the "bright" students. And parents can become quite frustrated, wondering why their intelligent children now receive such poor grades and hate school.

Teenagers are changing intellectually.

Social

Another area of great change is the social arena. First, let's consider friends.

In the Palm of My Hand

When I arrived at the classroom, a dozen junior highers were already there, talking, laughing, and poking one another—the usual. A quick survey of the room revealed that my assistants hadn't arrived, so I would be the only adult in the class. Knowing that it is virtually impossible to teach and keep order at the same time, I decided to scrap my lesson plan and, instead, try to keep everyone's attention with a dramatic retelling of the Bible story for that week.

We were studying Mark and had come to the end of Chapter 5. So I told the story of Jesus in the boat with the disciples when a huge storm engulfed them. With passion and expression, I set the scene—the raging storm, the disciples' fear, the disciples waking Jesus, and Jesus rebuking them and then calming the wind and the waves.

Everyone sat in rapt attention as I spoke, and I thought, *This is great, I have them in the palm of my hand! They really understand.* Then I began to relate the story at the beginning of Chapter 6. "After the storm died down, the disciples continued to the other side of the lake. But just as they got out of the boat, a wild man ran toward them! This man had lived in the cemetery. He was crazy and strong. In fact, broken chains were hanging from his wrists because, as the Bible says, 'No man could hold him.'"

"Why didn't they shoot him!" interjected a seventh-grade boy. Quickly an elder's son responded sarcastically, "They didn't have guns, stupid!"

Obviously confused, another seventh grader looked up at me, his eyes wide, and implored, "When did all this happen?"

—Dave Veerman

Usually young children find their playmates in the neighborhood—kids who live next door or down the street. Even in elementary school, most of the students will live fairly close to one another. In junior high or middle school, however, that begins to change. A typical junior high will have graduates of two or three elementary schools and, thus, many neighborhoods. The next building in the educational system, high school, draws students from an even wider geographical area, with two or three junior high schools feeding one high school. This factor alone precipitates changes in relationships.

At the same time, the other changes occurring in adolescent bodies and minds will have a strong effect on friendships, and kids will tend to gather in groups with similar interests. Also, during the junior high years, at the onset of puberty and sexual awareness, the wide variety of family values begins to show. For example, in a family where the parents are quite conservative, the junior high–age son may only be allowed to see G- and PG-rated movies. This boy's best friend, however, may be allowed to see PG-13 movies and occasionally one that is rated R—his parents don't see any problems with the language, sex, and violence. This difference will lead to interesting confrontations, especially when the two friends want to go to a movie together. Similar differences appear in clothing styles, music and entertainment choices, church attendance, and relationships with the opposite sex.

One parent explains: "Susie's best friend in grade school was Karin—she lived across the street. But in middle school, it became apparent that Karin's parents were much more permissive than we were. They seemed to encourage Karin's interest in boys and even had a boy-girl party. We found ourselves often on the defensive with Susie, trying to explain why we were 'so strict.' The biggest problem came in eighth grade when Karin's mother had to consistently work late. At least two days a week, Karin would be home alone, with no supervision. And she started having friends come over, including boys."

Adolescents are also very aware of the social pecking order, and most would love to be part of the "in crowd" of athletes, cheerleaders, and other social powerbrokers. We shouldn't underestimate the need for acceptance and push for popularity.

The second great change in relationships concerns the opposite sex. As mentioned earlier, puberty brings a growing awareness of and appreciation for the opposite sex. Early adolescents aren't sure how to relate and may act silly (writing names all over notebooks, sending notes, calling and talking endlessly about who's interested in whom) or use words and phrases that make them sound older (he's "going out" with her until she "dumps" him).

In high school, dating becomes a big issue—when to date, whom to date, what to do on a date, how to respond when you're asked out by the wrong person, and so forth. Young people can feel pressured from a number of sources, from their feelings to their friends, to become sexually active. This is another area where the parents' values come into play. Some parents push their kids to date early, while others insist that their teenagers wait.

In chapter 4, we will continue this discussion of relationships, and in chapter 10, we will discuss talking with teens about sex. The point here is that teens are changing dramatically in this area as well. And these changes, along with those in the other areas, can lead to turmoil and conflict.

WHAT TO DO

We can help our teenagers make a smooth transition into adulthood by how we treat them.

See Them as Young Adults

This won't be easy, but we should start thinking of and treating our teenagers more as young adults and less as overgrown children. This will be difficult because our teenagers have always been our children. We have baby pictures of them still on display around the house. We remember changing their diapers, wiping their noses, teaching them how to ride bikes. It's not easy to start thinking of these people as adults. These kids will always be our children, but if we treat them like young children, we will more than likely get childish behavior in response. We will stunt their growth. Parents who treat their teenager like a child should not be surprised when he or she acts like a three-year-old. Teenagers often do just that. Although they can act quite maturely around other adults who treat them with respect, they may revert back to being a young child when they are home because that's how they are treated at home. Teenagers will live up or down to whatever expectations we have of them. If we treat them like adults, they will act more like adults.

Understand and Help

Second, we can be understanding and helpful to our teenagers as they go through all this growing and changing. Stress can be minimized if teens know what to expect and have a positive attitude about their development. Puberty is an opportune time to talk with our kids about their physical and sexual development and to help them see all these changes as good, not bad. Girls should learn about and be prepared for the onset of menstruation, and boys should learn about ejaculation and be prepared for their first wet dream. Some kids are embarrassed or frightened by what is happening to them, and we can assure them that they are normal and that everything will be fine.

Everything Is Growing and Changing!

Every day, just about, something new seems to be happening to this body of mine and I get scared sometimes. I'll wake up in the middle of the night and I can't go back to sleep and I toss and I turn and I can't stop my mind. It's racing fast and everything is coming into it and I think of my two best friends and now their faces are all broken out and I worry mine will break out too, but so far it hasn't, and I think of my sizes and I can't get it out of my head—the chest size and the stomach size and what I'll be wearing and whether I'll be able to fit into this kind of dress or the latest swimsuit. Well it goes on and on and I'm dizzy, even though it's maybe one o'clock in the morning and there I am, in bed, so how can you be dizzy?

Everything is growing and changing. I can see my mother watching me. I can see everyone watching me. There are times I think I see people watching me when they really couldn't care less! My dad makes a point of not looking, but he catches his look, I guess. I'm going to be "big-chested." That's how my mother describes herself! I have to figure out how to dress so I feel better—I mean, so I don't feel strange, with my bosom just sticking out at everyone. I have to decide if I should shave my legs. I will—but I just wish I could go back to being a little girl, without all these problems and these decisions!

My brother isn't doing too good either. He's got acne and he can't shave without hurting himself because of all those pimples. He doesn't like an electric shaver; he says they don't feel clean to his face. He's a nut about taking showers. Two a day! He's always using deodorant. He's got all that hair under his arms. So do I! We will have our "buddy talks" and a lot of the time we just ask,

"When will it end—so we can just have a body that looks the same from one week to the next?"

From an interview with a young adolescent girl in Robert Coles and Geoffrey Stokes, *Sex and the American Teenager* (New York: Harper & Row, 1985), 33.

Create Healthy Rites of Passage

Third, we should create healthy and positive rites of passage for our kids. We can be creative here, perhaps having a celebration when a child reaches a milestone or a certain age or grade in school. One church has a mentoring program for eighth graders where each student is paired with an adult. For two or three months, the mentors and their students regularly meet, one-on-one, to go through specific material designed by the youth director. At the end of this process and the school year, the mentors and their students are honored in a worship service. This has taken the place of the confirmation classes and has proved to be a very meaningful rite of passage into high school.

Work Ourselves Out of a Job

We want our kids to grow up, to move out of the house and into lives of their own. This can be accomplished by giving them increased freedom, privileges, and responsibilities as they grow and mature. During a one-on-one breakfast or lunch, we could talk this through and list our expectations for each other.

On the eve of each of his son's birthdays starting at age eleven, one father would take his son out for dinner, just the two of them. After the meal, he would draw a box, and in the box he would write the new allowance amount, privileges, curfew times, and other pertinent information and expectations for the coming year. The next year, this father would bring out the drawing of the box from the previous year and draw another, bigger box around it, illustrating the ever-increasing amount of freedom the son gained with every passing year. The box symbolized limits, but it also demonstrated the father's expectations for his son's growth and increased maturity.

Teenagers are in transition from childhood to adulthood. Let's help the transition be smooth.

Rites of Passage?

- Having new responsibilities at home
- Getting an allowance or a checking account
- Going to a Promise Keepers rally with Dad
- Having a weekly breakfast or lunch out with Mom or Dad
- Getting new bedroom furniture
- Taking guitar lessons
- Getting a love note from Mom or Dad
- Going on an overnight fishing trip with Dad
- Taking a weekend or summer job
- Being allowed to wear makeup
- Getting a driver's license
- Teaching a Sunday school class
- Receiving flowers
- Buying a suit
- Being allowed to stay at home without a baby- or house-sitter
- Going to a ladies' tea with Mom

THINK IT THROUGH

1. What's your most painful memory from sixth through ninth grades? What's the most positive experience during those years that you can remember?
2. What emotional baggage do you still carry from those years?
3. When did you experience your growth spurt? What effects did your size have on your involvement in sports? . . . with the opposite sex? . . . with being popular?
4. Who was your favorite teacher in junior high? Why?
5. When did you discover that you could think and understand?
6. Who was your best friend in elementary school? In junior high school? In high school? What caused your friendships to change?
7. What frustrates you the most about your teenagers' friends? How did your parents feel about your friends at that age?
8. Who formed the "in crowd" at your high school? What did you do to become more popular?
9. What did your parents do to help you through these years of transition?
10. What can you do to enhance your teenagers' self-concept?
11. What can you do to treat your teenagers more like adults?

Chapter 3

Teens Are Seeking Autonomy

To be perfectly honest, Ruth, I'm confused." Liz spoke slowly. She had called Ruth to discuss the upcoming block party, but when Ruth asked about Emily, the conversation had taken a turn away from the neighborhood social event to a very personal and, at times, painful topic. Liz continued. "Emily and I used to have such a good relationship, and she was always so sweet, kind, and cooperative. But lately she seems to argue with me over everything and is even defiant. When she gets home, she goes right to her room and shuts the door—it's like she wants to shut us out of her life. And when we drive her to school, we have to drop her off a block away because she doesn't want to be seen with us. Bob and I don't know what to do."

Liz and Bob face a common dilemma. Most parents of teenagers struggle with this 180 degree change in attitude. And it's not just the junior high negativity where everything is said to be "stupid," "dumb," or "boring." It's our high school students who seem to want to separate themselves from the rest of the family and have nothing to do with us.

If that's the case in your home, relax—it's normal.

SEARCH FOR IDENTITY

Teenagers need to determine who they are, and they want to make a life of their own.

According to Erik Erikson's classic stages of psychological development, the psychological-emotional focus of children in the "school age" (approximately ages six to twelve) is "industry versus inferiority." "Industry" means feeling competent. That is, a child needs to feel that he or she is good at something. Thus, those who work with early adolescents (approximately ages eleven to fourteen) teach skills to their students, especially life skills, realizing their students' needs and interests.

In Erikson's next stage, "adolescence" (approximately ages thirteen to eighteen), the focus is "identity versus confusion." Here the young person is working on his or her self-concept and answering the questions, Who am I? and Where do I fit in? Teens need to find a self that they can live with.

During this search, they may experiment with many "selves," assuming various identity roles. For example, they might try on athlete or cheerleader and work at being popular. Or they might try on socialite and be the life of the party. Other possibilities include tough guy, rebel, intellectual, lover, musician, and actor. Another role competing for their attention is that of Christian, especially if they are active in church or a youth group. Every high school has a variety of roles and groups from which to choose. Kids can bounce among these roles for any number of reasons: They may want to be accepted by a group (as we'll see in chapter 4, they are looking for friends); they may have a special skill or talent; they may just like the attention they get. And these days, Internet chat rooms provide a place for teens to experiment with different "selves." It feels safer because there's no face-to-face rejection involved.

Sometimes young people are confused about how to combine some of these roles; for example, Christian and athlete or tough guy and intellectual. Trying to find one's identity can be very stressful for teens.

In this search for identity and drive for independence, teenagers want to separate themselves from their parents and create an identity of their own. This process is sometimes called "individuation"—when children try to establish their own personalities, likes and dislikes, behaviors and attitudes. They want to be themselves. As young children, they were little carbon copies of Mom and Dad, and they got their identity (and security) from being just like Mom or Dad. But things have changed, and now one thing's for sure—your son or daughter *doesn't want to be you anymore.*

This can be tough for parents to take, especially those who have enjoyed a close relationship with their children when they were younger. One father said, "I felt hurt when Julie [his fifteen-year-old daughter] didn't want me to hug her anymore. She would even push me away! I wondered what had happened to my little girl who used to crawl up on my lap and ask for hugs."

A mother explained, "People used to say how much my daughter, Jasmine, and I were alike. It was obvious that we had the same temperament and personality, even tastes in clothes and food. Then one day, out of the blue, Jasmine announced to me during an argument, *'I'm not like you, Mom!'* I didn't know what to think."

Fun

My eldest son had always encouraged me to be the room mom, go on the field trips, and so on until one day in junior high. He announced that he did *not* want me to chaperone the show choir bus. My husband knew that this change of behavior (Matthew seeking autonomy) was difficult for me. So he chose wonderful words to help me understand: "Matthew *knows* he can have fun with you along. Now he just wants to find out if he can have fun *without* you."

—Kendra Smiley

THE SIGNS

Because every person is unique, your children will hit this stage of life and push for independence at different times and with different symptoms. Some teens, like Julie, will be subtle, while others, like Jasmine, will be obvious and direct. Some may begin this push for independence at age eleven or twelve, while others may wait until they're fifteen, sixteen, or older. Whenever it occurs, however, here are some of the signs that your teenage son or daughter is seeking autonomy.

First, there's the need for *privacy*. This means shutting the door to one's room and having a private life that Mom and Dad don't know anything about. When kids are young, their parents usually know everything about them. Their lives are an open book—they share everything. But teenagers may have secrets and feel reluctant to tell their parents everything that is going on in their lives. This is not necessarily because they have anything terrible to hide. They just want privacy, a life of their own. This is normal and is rarely a cause for alarm. Of course, if a teenager's need for privacy results in negative manifestations such as sneaking out or lying, it may be necessary for parents to intervene. In most cases, however, it's best to respect the teen's need for privacy and to avoid overreacting.

Second, there are the *roles*, as described above. If your daughter is an extrovert, she may be on the phone constantly, lining up the right group to go to the game and planning the next party. If your son is a hopeful athletic star, he may want to hang out with the older players and buy a weight machine. For some, studies will fade in importance, while others will make them a priority. And each of these roles directly affects the wardrobe.

A third sign is *disengagement* from the family. Suddenly teenagers don't want to participate in family activities anymore, even family vacations and outings that they used to enjoy so much. Also, they don't want to eat dinner with the family. And they certainly don't want to be seen with their parents at school or other public places. That's why your son may ask (demand?) that you drop him off a block from school—he considers you to be hopelessly uncool and embarrassing.

The fourth sign, often related to the first three, is *conflict*. The discussions, heated arguments, disagreements, and battles with teenagers pushing for autonomy can be very mild or quite severe. But conflict is a normal and sometimes necessary part of the process of separation. In fact, a group of sociologists studying families of primates found that even adolescent chimpanzees appear to need conflict (fighting) with their parents as they get older. The scientists concluded that without conflict, the young *might never leave the nest!*

While a comparison between primates and humans may be interesting (if not particularly comforting), it probably isn't very helpful. The conflict we experience with our kids is rarely a positive experience and more likely is discouraging and damaging to relationships in the family.

Still, parental conflict with teenagers comes with the territory, usually occurring in one of the following areas:

Power and Authority

"Mom, can I go with Jennifer and Cyndi to the mall after supper?"

"No, dear, you know you're not allowed out on a school night."

"But Mom, please. I'll be home by eight-thirty. I'll still have plenty of time to get all my homework done."

"No, Tammy. We don't want you out on school nights."

"Mom, you're not being fair. You let Jeremy do all kinds of stuff just because he's a boy."

"Jeremy is older, and besides, that has nothing to do with it. I said no, and that's final."

"You never let me do anything! Why? Why can't I go?"

"Tammy, you're starting to make me angry."

"You're getting angry? I'm the one who's not allowed to be with my friends! Why, Mom? You just like ruining my life!"

Sound familiar? Perhaps you've had a confrontation like this one that ended with Tammy in tears, sulking for the rest of the evening, and her mom in a very bad mood. The issue, of course, has less to do with the rightness or wrongness of going to the mall than it does with *who has the power.* This is an example of the classic power struggles that occur frequently in homes with teenagers.

Research has confirmed what most parents of teenagers instinctively know: The value that increases the most during adolescence is "to make my own decisions." Nothing becomes more important to a young adolescent than the acquisition of power. Little children have no power. They make very few decisions of their own. Mommy and Daddy (or other adults) make all their decisions for them—when to go to bed, when to get up, what to wear, what to eat, where to go, whom to play with, and so forth. Adults, on the other hand, make all (or most) of their decisions for themselves. This is what distinguishes a child from an adult!

It's not surprising, therefore, that children who are becoming adults (adolescents) covet that one characteristic that differentiates a child from an adult—*power*. They don't want all the power, just some of it. They want to make their own decisions, *now*, in the areas mentioned above: when to go to bed, what to wear, what to eat, where to go, what to do, and whom to do it with.

Conflict occurs, of course, when parents refuse to give up any of that power and authority. Arguments arise and emotional tug of wars develop. "You will do what I tell you to do . . . *because I'm the parent, that's why!*" That statement makes perfectly good sense to parents, but it seems unreasonable and unfair to teenagers, who can't understand why they can't make their own decisions—or at least some of them.

If seeking autonomy and independence is a primary task of adolescence (it is), then letting go of children is the primary task for parents of teenagers. In a few short years, our teenagers will be on their own, and once out in the world, they must be able to survive. Gradually, whether they seem ready or not, our kids will need to take over the controls of their own lives. But allowing them to do this is not easy. The deepest impulse of parents screams out against this duty: "They are too young! They don't know what they're doing! The world is different today—it's so much more complicated, tough, and dangerous. And besides, I'm pretty good at making decisions. I can make better decisions than they can."

Still, parents must let go. And, to make matters even trickier, they must do so while still being parents: setting limits, being responsible for the teenager, making demands. Often the most difficult task for the parents of a demanding teenager is to show love and respect for him or her.

> Our need is to be needed. Their need is to not need us.
>
> —Wayne Rice

Behavior

"Jason, I thought I told you to clean your room!"

"I did."

"It's just as messy as it was."

"No, it's not. Anyway, this is the way I like it."

"Clean your room. Now!"

"But I already did."

"Either you clean your room before suppertime, or I'll come in there and clean it for you! And believe me, you don't want me going through all your stuff. I may just throw a lot of it away."

"You stay out of my room! I'll clean it when I feel like it."

"Don't you dare tell me what to do!"

"Well it's my room and I like it this way!"

The crazy thing is—Jason really does like his room that way. It's his way of saying, "I'm not my parents." You may have decorated your home in Early American, but your teenager has opted for Early Landfill. It drives you crazy. It's embarrassing. It's possibly unhealthy. You imagine that ten or twenty years from now, you will visit his home and find dirty underwear and half-eaten, maggot-infested sandwiches lying on the living room floor. You are convinced that he'll never learn to pick up after himself.

More often than not, however, kids grow up and become more like their parents than they ever imagined they would. In the meantime, during their days at home, they feel compelled to assert themselves and to act and behave in ways that identify them as different from Mom and Dad. This may take the form of rebellion, but it doesn't have to.

Some people believe that all teenagers rebel. But rebellion is a strong word, usually signifying behavior that is extreme and destructive. Not all teenagers rebel, *but every teenager has a need to assert himself or herself*—to behave differently from his or her parents. Again, this can be quite subtle, or it can be outrageous.

You probably did the same thing when you were a teenager, fighting with your parents over which radio station to listen to in the car or arguing over the length of your hair. Your parents insisted that you wear a coat and tie to church, but your idea of "dressing up" was to wear clean Levi's and the new T-shirt you got at the rock concert last week. Remember the conflict?

Derek, a junior in high school and a talented artist and avid fisherman, wanted to paint his room, almost like a mural. Wisely his parents gave their OK. Now visitors to this young man's bedroom enter an underwater scene, complete with large fish on all four walls and a giant squid hanging from the ceiling.

Janine is a good student who has immersed herself in politics. While her parents are conservative Republicans, Janine has become the family liberal, supporting many radical causes and campaigning for candidates on the left. Dinnertimes feature some lively discussions, to say the least.

On the other hand, many teenagers assert themselves by smoking and exhibiting other antisocial or antiestablishment behaviors. Studies confirm that teenagers continue to smoke cigarettes despite the antitobacco mood of our society and the evidence that smoking causes a host of terrible problems and diseases. We shouldn't be surprised at this—smoking is an easy way for teenagers to show that they are independent and *not* going along with what adults say or think.

A Modern-Day Proverb

When your children become teenagers, they will fire you as a parent but hire you back as a consultant.

Our teenagers will find some creative ways to let us know that they are not us. This is guaranteed to be aggravating and perhaps even a little disturbing. But the capacity to let go—to allow our kids to be themselves instead of us—is crucial to being the parent of a teenager. While we can guide, direct, and influence, we must somehow accept that it will be almost impossible to force teenagers to be what they don't want to be. If our teenagers are demonstrating the generally uncooperative and independent behavior that is the hallmark of adolescence, it is wise to do what we can to restrict the conflict, hang in there, and love our kids in spite of it all. During adolescence, teenagers begin to resemble the adults they will eventually become, and the initial indicators may not be what we had envisioned. We may want to change what we see. In most cases, however, it's better to accept our teenagers for who they are than to punish them for not being somebody else (us).

Whether over power and authority or over specific behaviors, certainly this drive for autonomy will lead to conflict.

WHAT TO DO

When kids change from innocent babies to cynical and sarcastic teenagers, and from cute, cuddly, and dependent "I love you, Mommy and Daddy" children to snarly, independent "I hate this family" adolescents, parents can become frustrated, nervous, and outright hostile. In addition to questioning our parenting ability, we may find ourselves yelling at these older children even though we really do love them dearly. Instead of losing our cool and our confidence, here are ways to respond.

First, *we shouldn't take it personally* when our teenagers decide that they don't want to be like us anymore. This, of course, is easier said than done, especially when our kids act as though they are repelled by us. Sometimes teenagers seem to be totally allergic to parents.

If a parent walks into the TV room and innocently asks, "What are you watching?" the teenager may get up without a word, go to his or her room, and turn on the stereo, apparently to not have to be in the same room with the parent. At the mall, the teenager (who needed a ride and money for clothes) may insist on meeting Mom or Dad at the car at a designated time. The message that comes through loud and clear is rejection: "You are hopelessly uncool. You are an embarrassment to me."

We shouldn't take any of this personally. In reality, conflict is raging inside our teenagers. Down deep, they are attracted to their parents, love their parents, and want closeness. But their drive for independence and autonomy causes them to resist these urges and push away. Of course, because of nature and nurture, the kids will probably come back and end up very similar to their parents in their values and views. But right now, during adolescence, they need to find themselves and to be themselves.

The process of leaving the nest requires separation. It happens in all families, even the best ones—and it's necessary.

Second, *we should find creative ways to stay close.* Separation and closeness are not opposites but two sides of the same coin. We need to find new ways to stay close—ways that are different from those we used when the children were young. More adultlike ways to spend time together could include sharing a hobby, working on a home remodeling project, taking a special trip, working out or running a marathon, going out on a "date," and so on. Generally speaking, the key here is to find ways to stay close while allowing the teen some distance.

Use imagination when planning vacations and other family trips and outings. Think of creative ways to make these events tolerable and even enjoyable for a young, emerging adult. For example, you could let your teenager bring a friend along for the week at the cottage. Or on the trip to Grandma's house, you could suggest a side trip to a site that your son or daughter would really like to visit (Hard Rock Cafe, Rock 'n' Roll Hall of Fame, a professional sporting event, a concert by a favorite group, the world's largest mall or amusement park, and so forth). Planning the family vacation *with* your teenager will give him or her ownership and a desire to make the best of it.

Give Me Liberty . . . Or Whatever

Teenagers truly believe that they absolutely do not want controls, and that without them they would do just fine. In reality, controls do act as a source of *unacknowledged* security for them. Total responsibility for one's life is a burden. With total freedom a person has to bear the full brunt of worrying about making the right decisions. There is something nice and secure (though, at another level, also infuriating) in the knowledge that there are one or two adults around who are *also* making decisions about what is best for you. Without this guidance the full burden of responsibility could cause more stress than most teenagers can or wish to handle. It's hard enough being a teenager without having to take on the entire responsibility for your own welfare.

Anthony E. Wolf, *Get Out of My Life, but First Could You Drive Me and Cheryl to the Mall?: A Parent's Guide to the New Teenager* (New York: Noonday Press, 1992), 59.

Third, *we should respect our teenagers' privacy.* This means knocking on the closed bedroom door when we want to talk and resisting the temptation to go through the desk and dresser drawers or read the diary. When the door is shut, we shouldn't assume the worst. The shut door is mostly an innocent symbol of autonomy. It says, "This is my territory. You must be invited in or ask permission to enter here."

Having said this, however, please don't think that the desire for privacy means that teenage children should be allowed to do anything they want behind closed doors. Too many parents, in an attempt to be socially and psychologically correct, have closed their eyes and ears to immoral and self-destructive behavior. Some teens have used drugs, had sex, and worse (some have even committed suicide) in their rooms while their parents were home. Remember—you are still the parent and you have responsibility for your children. It is your house, and you have the right to go into any room if you feel it is necessary. Your teenagers need to know what kind of behavior you expect and permit and that while you respect their right to privacy, you also reserve the right to inspect any room anytime you feel it is warranted. By not acting on that right, you communicate trust and respect to your teenager.

Generally speaking, the only time parents should exercise their right to invade their teens' privacy is when they have a good reason to believe that the teenagers are concealing behavior that is immoral or harmful. Otherwise, they should let them be alone when they want to be alone.

Fourth, *we should allow our teenagers to take more responsibility for making their own decisions.* A wise saying is instructive here: "When your children get older, start letting out more rope . . . but not so much that they will hang themselves."

One thing we don't want to be is "permissive parents." While we want to allow our kids to have more and more power and control over their lives as they get older, we still need to set limits and then enforce those limits by providing logical consequences (see chapter 11), at least until they are on their own. Parents have the right to make demands that are reasonable for the welfare of the whole family.

As we begin allowing our teenagers to make more of their own decisions, we can help them to make good ones. For example, you could allow your son or daughter to buy a new stereo. As your teenager decides which one to buy, you can demonstrate how to use a problem-solving grid, where to find information on the various brands (perhaps from *Consumer*

The Church Problem

When our son Nathan was about sixteen years old, we had a hard time keeping him interested in church. He simply didn't want to go. The small church we attended was boring to him, and none of his friends went there.

So, we decided to "let out some rope" rather than using rope to drag him to church every Sunday with us. This was not easy for us to do.

We told Nathan first of all that church attendance was not optional in our family. As long as he lived in our house, he would be in church on Sunday. That was non-negotiable, and we made sure he understood that.

But we also let him know that we couldn't force him to attend *our* church. We expressed our faith in his ability to take responsibility for his own spiritual growth: "Nate, if you don't like our church, then pick one. There are plenty of good churches in our city. Take the car and go. We will support you in that."

We didn't think he would actually do it, but he did. He chose to go to a church where many of his friends went—a church of a denomination different from ours. Frankly, it broke our hearts. It was embarrassing. People would ask us, "Where's Nate?" We hated to tell them that he was going to that "other" church down the street.

But it wasn't a bad church. And Nate became enthusiastic about church again. We never had to remind him to go. And when we all got home on Sunday afternoon, we were able to share our respective church experiences with one another. It was wonderful to hear what he was doing and how his faith was taking shape. We even argued a little about theology. Nate got very involved in the youth group at that "other" church and later went into youth ministry himself, thanks largely to the mentoring he received there.

Is this something you should try? Maybe, maybe not. But it sure shows how a little rope can make a lot of difference.

—Wayne and Marci Rice

Reports or on the Internet), and how to shop around for the best deal. Those are important skills to learn. But remember—when you let out the rope, don't keep pulling it back in. It's tempting to say to the teenager, "You can make your own decisions, as long as you make the ones that I approve."

If the decision is too dangerous to allow for mistakes, then we shouldn't let the teenager make it in the first place. If it isn't, then we should allow the teen to make his or her decision and live with it. We will need to live with it, too, and resist the temptation to fix mistakes. As kids experience the consequences of their decisions, they learn how to make good ones.

Finally, *we should allow kids to assert themselves in harmless ways.* As we discussed earlier, our teenagers will probably want to act and behave in ways that express their emerging adulthood. As long as the behavior is not harmful or morally wrong, it's generally recommended that we allow it. This strategy may prevent harmful, destructive rebellion later on. Allowing teens to assert themselves in harmless ways reduces their need to rebel.

It's much easier to write and say this than to do it, of course, especially if the teenager wants to do something that we don't like or even find repulsive. For example, many teens today like to experiment with extremes in hair color or with body piercing. While these behaviors are not lethal (hair will grow back to its

Assertion

Which of the following would you consider to be less harmful ways for your teenagers to assert themselves?

- Hairstyle
- Clothing and accessories
- Music and entertainment
- Hobbies
- Study habits
- Ear or body piercing
- Choice of TV shows
- Hair color
- Bedroom decor
- Work habits
- Eating habits
- Favorite sports teams
- Tattoos
- Political views
- Worship style

original color and holes in the skin can heal up), you may want to work out a compromise solution with your son or daughter and set some limits. Sometimes you can postpone (or even discourage completely) certain behaviors by setting limits on *when* your kids can do certain things. For example, you can compromise with your son and allow him to dye his hair orange (or whatever color he chooses) during the summer. Or you might allow your daughter to get her navel pierced when she turns seventeen. Remember, eventually our kids will be able to do whatever they want whenever they want and there won't be anything we can do about it. It's best to be reasonable and understanding now and to allow our kids to separate. We don't have to *like* any of this. But by allowing it, we show faith in our kids and respect for their right to be who they want to be.

Teens are seeking autonomy. Our challenge is to stay close in spite of it, and to help them do it positively.

THINK IT THROUGH

1. When you were in high school, how did you see yourself? With what groups did you identify—who did you try to be?
2. How did you express your autonomy? How did your parents react to those expressions? In what ways did some of your friends rebel?
3. When did you first notice your children pushing for independence? How did you react?
4. In what areas have you and your teenagers had conflict over autonomy?
5. What can you do to make family vacations more fun for your teenagers?
6. What creative activity can you do with your teenagers to help you stay close during this stressful time of life?
7. What can you do to allow your teenagers to have more privacy?
8. What important decisions will you allow your teenagers to make this year? How about next year?
9. In what less-than-harmful ways would you allow your teenagers to assert their autonomy?

Chapter 4

Teens Are Expanding Their Relationships

The Parents of Teenagers adult Sunday school class promises to feature a lively discussion. Anticipating the advertised topic, "Friends or Foes, Our Kids' Changing Relationships," the classroom is buzzing with interesting and animated conversation.

"I noticed the change in fifth grade," states Marge Shaffer to Claudine Johnson as they enter the room. "Maddie would get on the phone as soon as she got home from school and would only get off if we made her. And she hasn't stopped—the phone seems to grow out of her head! And when she isn't talking on the phone, she runs to answer it whenever it rings."

"It's the same at our house," adds Jerry Roth, overhearing

Marge's comment. "Our Shannon almost lives on the phone. How can she and her friends find so much to talk about?"

Several steps away, next to the coffeepot, Mark and Phil's discussion takes a different route. "What worries me about Mark Jr. is his choice of friends. I've never met these boys, but I sure don't like what I've heard about some of them."

Nodding his head in agreement, Phil offers, "I know what you mean. Some of Tyler's friends are almost scary—the way they dress and all."

Nearby, in a circle of moms, the topic is fashion, fads, and being popular. No one is happy about the situation and the changes they've seen in their kids.

Regardless of background, race, economic status, family situation, political leanings, and strong opinions in other areas, all the parents in that class could agree on one important point— friends mean everything to teenagers!

And they're right. In fact, it would be fair to say that the three most important things to a teenager are: friends, friends, and friends.

When did you begin to notice the change in your son or daughter? Perhaps, like Marge, you saw this heightened interest in friends and relationships surface at about age ten or eleven when long telephone conversations became a daily routine. Or this change may not have hit your child until seventh grade or so. Or maybe in your family the change was nearly imperceptible, not a big deal; yet on closer examination, you realize that friends have become a critical component of your teenager's life.

Let's face it, every child is unique, and a number of factors play into an individual's need and desire for close relationships. For example, some people are extreme extroverts; that is, they are energized by people and parties. Others tend to be rather introverted and can survive and thrive being alone much of the time. Some families operate with frenetic energy—chaos seems to reign as friends treat the front entrance as a revolving door and the family room as a hangout. Other homes seem eerily quiet and calm. Regardless of the variables of personality type, temperament, and family system, however, adolescence brings a new emphasis on the social area of life. Little children need playmates; teenagers need friends.

I LIKE YOU

The most important question on the mind of adolescents is Do you like me? When they were very young, in warm and positive homes, they continually received an affirmative answer through words and actions from their parents: "We love you. You are wonderful. You are great . . . the best!" That was when they were children. But remember, adolescence is a time of great transition (see chapter 2), featuring a strong move toward autonomy (see chapter 3). Our kids are becoming adults, and they want to be treated like adults. So at this point in their lives they want to know, "Does anyone *outside my family* like me?" "Am I a likable person?" "What do *other people* think about me?"

A friend is someone who answers, "Yes. I like you. I want to be with you."

INTENSITY

Three strong forces intensify this push for friendships. It's important to understand these forces and work with them, not against them, as we help our teenagers build relationships.

We have a cartoon on our refrigerator that features a sad young boy and his mom. The mom asks, "What's wrong?"

The boy replies, "Nobody likes me."

The mom tries to comfort her son: "That's not true. I like you," she says.

The boy replies, "Of course you do. . . . That's your job."

—Kendra Smiley

Survival

The first of these forces is survival, the drive to stay alive socially.

If you progressed through the public school system as you were growing up, you know that each new school became larger and drew from a wider geographical area. For example, you may have walked a few blocks to the elementary school with about three hundred other children. (Many elementary schools are K–6 and draw from one neighborhood or subdivision.) For junior high or middle school (grades 6 through 8), however, you may have had to ride a bike or take the school bus; these schools each draw from a larger geographical area, fed by two or three elementary schools, and usually range from five hundred to a thousand students. Finally, your high school may have been twice the size of your junior high, drawing students from all over town, and you probably had to drive or be driven there. Do you remember those first junior high and senior high days? Your emotional mix probably included fear.

A new school can be intimidating, especially when it is filled mostly with strangers. And with families moving so much these days, children confront this challenge much more often than we did at that age. Faced with the huge school and so many new people, kids will often cluster into small groups of friends. These student circles act like wolf packs (especially in junior high), fiercely protecting those on the inside and attacking those on the outside. This helps to explain why early adolescents can be so cruel to each other with their cutting comments. A tight group of friends provides protection and security, helping a young person make it through the school year.

Every person, of any age, has a basic need to be accepted and liked, to be loved. And most people avoid pain and rejection. It hurts to be ostracized, ignored, left out, or ridiculed. Yet that becomes routine in most junior high and high schools, as though it's part of the curriculum—"Ridicule 101" or "Basic

A Safe Place

Wise and effective teachers, coaches, and youth leaders will insist that their classes, teams, and youth groups be emotionally and physically safe places. This will mean . . .

- forbidding verbal put-downs, especially those based on race, religion, physical characteristics, family, or culture.

- developing a welcoming and positive atmosphere.

- defining limits and demanding discipline.

- demonstrating acceptance and love within those limits.

- affirming each person's strengths and important contributions.

- giving everyone the opportunity to achieve.

- motivating each person to do his or her best.

Cliques." Kids figure this out very quickly and make aggressive moves to fit in to the crowd and to be popular. That's one reason why kids are so preoccupied with their looks and their clothes. Their acceptance is at stake.

The right friends can help teens survive in a threatening environment.

Identity

As we discussed in chapter 3, the emotional-psychological focus of middle adolescents is the search for identity. This is the second strong force that directly affects the adolescent's choice of friends.

Typical high school students are trying to discover themselves; that is, they are attempting to answer the question Who is the *real* me? This search will involve trying on a variety of roles, assuming various identities in order to find a good fit. The search can be difficult and painful, especially when coupled with deep disappointment.

Consider Kristy, for example. She started playing soccer in kindergarten and continued to play through elementary school, nearly year-round. Agile, quick, and coordinated, Kristy could run circles around most of the other girls and usually reigned as her team's top scorer. But then, during seventh grade, Kristy grew several inches and, as a consequence, struggled with her coordination. She still was one of the better players on the team but was no longer the "star." Two years later, in high school, several other girls had passed Kristy in both speed and skill; as a result, soccer became more work than fun for her. After Kristy's sophomore year, she decided not to even try out for the team the next season. You can imagine the devastating effect this dramatic slide in her athletic achievements had on Kristy's self-concept. Change the name and the activity and this story could be retold in most homes: the junior high football star who stopped growing and found himself sitting on the bench; the straight-A student who struggled in geometry and lost interest in school; the musical lead whose voice changed; the fun-loving jokester who became devastated by a personal tragedy at home. Self-concepts can take a beating at this age.

Each of these high school identity roles has a group of young people who think and feel that way about themselves. These kids will clump together because they are (or want to be) football players, dancers, computer geeks, actors, burnouts, "gangstas," techies, musicians, intellectuals, or whatever. Ethnic, cultural, and religious commonalities can also draw students together (especially in our pluralistic society—see chapter 1).

The push for identity pulls young people toward one another. In fact, an analysis of a high school student's friends will reveal much about that student's self-concept.

Independence

The third strong force that affects friendships is the push for autonomy.

As we discussed in chapter 3, this drive for independence often leads to conflict over who makes decisions. Friendships can be a lightning rod for this conflict because choosing one's own friends is an important symbol of independence, especially when parents seem to be threatened by those friends.

- When Dad says something like, "I don't like that boy. You can do better than that!" the teenage son thinks and often says, "Oh yeah? You don't even know him. You always put my friends down. You can't tell me what to do!"

- When parents say, "What's wrong with the kids at church?" the teenager laughs and thinks, *What's wrong with the kids at school?*
- When Mom says, "I don't want you seeing her anymore—I forbid you!" the teenage daughter stomps to her room, slams the door, and thinks, *You can't stop me! I'll see her in class!*

Each teenager's response in these examples shouts autonomy. When parents question friendship choices, a frequent response is, "They are *my* friends!" emphasizing the personal decision, the personal choice.

A teen's declaration of independence is often written in his or her choice of friends.

OUTSIDE THE HOME

Clearly, teenagers need relationships outside the home. Not only is this what they want, but it is also healthy and good.

Certainly parents would like their children to develop into their close friends as adults. This can happen, eventually, if the relationship is built on a solid foundation. But first, separation must take place. If we knew of an otherwise healthy thirty-year-old who still lived with his parents and was totally dependent on them for food, clothing, shelter, and emotional support, we would conclude that something was wrong, that the relationship was sick.

The same is true socially. Children need to grow up and become independent of their parents in every area. That involves having close relationships outside the home. But this road to independence can be bumpy.

My Kid Doesn't Have Any Friends

While it is true that "friends are the lifeblood of adolescence," it is also true that some kids have a hard time finding or making friends. Many parents worry because their teens seem to be loners and don't desire or seek out friendships. This is troubling because almost all parents want their kids to be popular, to be liked by others. Sometimes parents see this as a validation of themselves. If my kid is popular, they reason, that means I've done a good job raising a likable, socially acceptable person.

There are many good reasons why some kids may be slow to develop relationships outside the home. Finding friends is not necessarily instant or easy. Kids tend to gravitate toward others who share their interests, and it may take some time to find the right group.

Some kids are naturally shy and are afraid to join a group for fear of rejection. Others aren't sure they fit in with any group just yet. They would rather just have one or two close friends to spend all their time with. Some teenagers are thoughtful and introverted and don't need validation from a group. This is not necessarily bad or a problem that needs to be solved. What is important, however, is that the teenager feels comfortable with him- or herself.

Adults who need friends and popularity to feel good about themselves may push their teenagers into having friends when they don't really need them. It's a mistake to force teenagers into relationships that they don't want or aren't ready for.

On the other hand, some teenagers are loners because they are perceived by others as rejects, outcasts, or nerds. You probably recall feeling sorry for the poor kid who was the butt of everyone's jokes and had to eat lunch alone. Maybe this person walked funny, talked funny, had a physical handicap of some kind, or just seemed like a "weirdo." It can be a terrible experience for a young person to suffer that kind of rejection and often even tougher for his or her parents.

What can parents do for a teenager in such a position? Here are some suggestions:

Give plenty of love and acceptance at home. Kids who are liked by their parents are more liable to be liked by others. Conversely, "outcast" kids usually believe that their parents do not really approve of them. Kids who enter their teen years feeling uncomfortable with themselves are prime targets for those kids who put others down in order to feel superior. We can provide our kids with the inner resources they need to avoid rejection by not rejecting them ourselves. This doesn't mean we have to approve of everything they do, of course, but we should avoid communicating that they disappoint us. We'll discuss this more in chapter 8.

Avoid being critical. The last thing that friendless teenagers need is criticism about it from their parents. Usually this only makes matters worse. Pushing teenagers to be more outgoing will sometimes just cause them to withdraw even farther. Just because a teenager seems to have no friends right now doesn't mean that the situation will stay that way forever. Sometimes kids need some time and space to be themselves. Rather than criticizing our teenagers for not having friends, we should encourage them to pursue interests they enjoy. They will probably discover others who like to do the same things, and they'll make some friends.

Avoid being a social planner. Do not force teens to enter into social situations and relationships. We shouldn't make them go to that party or activity if they really don't feel comfortable there. When teenagers are ready to participate in activities or make new friends, they will. Interfering only signals to them that we have no faith in them, and that will make them all the more resistant to change.

Be sensitive to problems that might benefit from intervention. A teenager might need help overcoming a specific problem that causes rejection from other people. For example, if a teenager habitually offends others by being rude or insensitive or needs to learn better grooming habits, some coaching might be in order. The teenager who has a weight problem, grossly crooked teeth, or a speech impediment could use help from Mom and Dad. Sometimes teens don't know how to correct a problem that interferes with their ability to make friends. We're not talking about cosmetic surgery or other superficial attempts to enhance appearance. The goal here is to do whatever is possible to correct undeniable problems that destroy self-esteem and act as barriers to positive relationships. When teenagers feel better about themselves, they will likely have an easier time making friends.

WHAT TO DO

Realizing the importance of friends and teenagers' need to develop strong relationships outside the home and understanding the other strong forces that affect adolescent friendships, here's how we can help smooth the way. These suggestions include two *don'ts*, actions and attitudes we should avoid, and seven *dos*, actions we should take.

Don'ts

First, *we shouldn't try to choose our kids' friends for them.* In other words, we shouldn't say something like: "Why don't you like John?" or "I want you to be friends with Mary!" Imagine someone saying that to you—it certainly wouldn't work, and you'd probably think, *I'll choose my own friends, thank you!* That approach won't be any more successful with our teenagers. We can, however, set some guidelines and perhaps rules for friendships—*before* they develop. One couple have this rule for their teenage son governing his choice of friends: "You are absolutely not allowed to hang out with anyone who smokes cigarettes, uses drugs, or has a police record."

Reach Out

Get to know your children's friends. The easiest way to do this is to make your home adolescent friendly. This includes stocking the refrigerator and pantry with soft drinks and snack foods, providing a place for them to watch television, play games, fool around with the computer, and listen to music. It also means generally being relaxed about your furniture and carpet. In short, it means making your home a place where your kids would want to bring their friends. When the friends do come over, show sincere interest in each one and treat them with respect. The results will be worth your investment of money and time.

Dave Veerman, *Ozzie & Harriet Had a Scriptwriter* (Wheaton, IL: Tyndale, 1996), 20.

Second, *we shouldn't fear our kids' friends.* At least, we shouldn't prejudge them. Just because the friends don't look like us or come from the same side of the tracks doesn't mean that they are evil and will lead our kids astray. Teens experiment with different kinds of friendships to find out where they fit in best. Actually, we probably had friends as teenagers whom we wouldn't want our kids to have. We survived, and chances are pretty good that our kids will too. (Some parents fear that their kids will make friends with *our* teenagers.)

Those are the two "don'ts." Now let's look at the positive side, how we can be proactive in the area of friendships.

Dos

First, *we should allow our teenagers to find and make friends.* Even though we can't choose whom our kids will connect with, we can allow and even encourage them to find and make friends. This can be a very positive experience during adolescence, and often these friendships will last a lifetime. High school reunions illustrate how much fun it can be to reconnect with old buddies after years of separation. Many people are surprised to discover how much those relationships meant back then (and often still do today).

Don't worry if your teenager seems to be something of a loner. Some kids need lots of friends while others need very few. (See the "My Kid Doesn't Have Any Friends" sidebar in this chapter.)

Second, *we should do all we can to give our teenagers a high view of themselves.* The best way to keep kids from falling in with the "wrong crowd" is to treat them with respect and dignity. Teenagers with a healthy dose of self-respect will be less likely to choose friends who will drag them down or demean them. As noted earlier, most kids choose friends from the crowd where they feel most comfortable, most accepted. A young person who feels like a loser tends to gravitate to others who perceive themselves as losers. Most kids who join gangs or get involved in other harmful behaviors have low self-esteem. They act tough or rebellious as a way of compensating for their lack of self-respect. They don't see themselves as having a future, so they live for the present. And the gang accepts them and gives them a place to belong.

Guide, Don't Block

An important principle in dealing with teenagers in many areas is "Guide, don't block." Take music, for example. Instead of forbidding the fourteen-year-old to listen to B-97,* explain calmly that you don't appreciate the dirty-talking, envelope-pushing D.J.s on that particular station, and perhaps Z-99* would be a better choice. (Note: Both stations play the same kind of music, but Z-99 is clean.) This way, your teen will understand that you aren't blasting his or her music but have other concerns.

We can use the same approach with friends. Let's say your daughter's best friend has shown some pretty disturbing behavior and attitudes lately and is obviously becoming a bad influence. Instead of listing in great detail all your problems with the friend and then forbidding your daughter to ever see her again, you can look for the opportunity to *guide* her elsewhere. At a down time in this relationship, for example, you could console your daughter and share with her the importance of having *several* close friends (not just one). Then you could brainstorm together about where she might find others, in *addition* to this one friend, not *instead* of her.

Guide, don't block.

*Fictitious stations—fill in the call letters and numbers from your community.

On the other hand, teenagers who are well adjusted and have a positive view of themselves tend to choose friends who are like themselves. We can't control our teenagers' choice of friends, but we can be their "mirrors." How they see themselves reflected through us will influence their relationships.

Third, *we should support the church's youth ministry.* This assumes, of course, that the church has a youth ministry—with strong adult leadership and a good variety of activities. Some parents seem to have an adversarial relationship with their youth pastor, criticizing aspects of the program or blaming him or her for problems they are having with their teenager (as if it were the youth pastor's job to "fix" their kid). Instead, we should be advocates for solid youth ministry in the church and community and volunteer to work behind the scenes to encourage and support our youth workers.

One of the main goals of youth ministry in the church is to provide a place for teens to make friends (both peer friends and adult friends) who share similar values and beliefs. We should support this ministry with prayer, financial help or other resources (refreshments, home, car, camcorder, boat, camping equipment), and our involvement whenever it is requested or needed. We can't force our teenagers to make Christian friends, but we can do much to help the youth ministry be successful.

If your church doesn't have a youth group or seems to care little about teenagers, perhaps you can help get something started. If that's not possible, you may have to find a church with a strong youth ministry. Recent studies have found that if teenagers have at least one friend who shares their values and faith and will stand with them against the crowd, they will be much less likely to give in to negative peer pressure and much more likely to take a stand for Christ. That's why it's so important to help our kids find friends in the family of faith.

Fourth, *we should be friendly toward our teenagers' friends.* At the very least, we shouldn't prejudge them or put them down. When parents criticize teenagers' friends, the teenagers take the criticism personally, as though Mom and Dad were also criticizing them. Young people understandably get upset with parents who put down their friends without knowing much about them. We know that it isn't fair to judge others on their looks or on others' assumptions—we don't like being treated that way. We should remember that fact when we are tempted to judge our teenagers' friends. Instead of prejudging, we should get to know them.

We shouldn't encroach on those friendships, of course, but we can welcome our kids' friends into our homes and let them know that we are glad they are there. We can invite them to have dinner, to stay overnight, or to participate in a family activity or outing. These acts will influence our teenagers to choose friends who are more compatible with the whole family.

We should also make our homes inviting to teenagers—places where they will want to hang out. (If there's food, they *will* come.) The slight wear and tear on the carpet and furniture is a small price to pay for knowing where our kids are and whom they are with. If possible, we should provide opportunities in our homes for our kids to have fun. Some families have made major changes, like installing a basketball hoop in the driveway, a swimming pool in the backyard, or a game room in the basement. If the house can handle it, host a few parties (see the "Let's Party" sidebar in this chapter for some guidelines). One family converted the garage into their Yes Room, where almost anything was permitted. The room didn't have carpet— just a drain in the middle of the floor. Being friendly toward our teenagers' friends doesn't have to be expensive to pay off.

Fifth, *we should get to know the parents of our teenagers' friends.* The school or church youth ministry may have a way to make this happen through a PTA group, a parents' support group, or a class like the one mentioned at the beginning of this chapter. It's just as important to know the parents of our kids' friends now as it was when they were in elementary school. Chances are we will discover that other parents share many of our feelings and agree with our decisions about parenting. Sometimes teenagers can make their parents feel as though they are the only ones in the world with rules.

Sixth, *we should talk with our teenagers about friends*, helping them understand what a friend is and what a friend is not. We can help them see that not all friendships are for life, that all relationships have an ebb and flow, and that friends come and go. Sometimes friends disappoint us, and sometimes they hurt us. This is normal and should be expected. Usually kids are relieved to hear this because they have unrealistic expectations of friendships.

Seventh, *we should help our teenagers find some adult friends.* Teenagers need adult friends outside the home to affirm them, to offer counsel and advice, and to serve as role models and mentors. This is especially true with the demise of the extended family (see chapter 1). Youth ministry can play an important role here—professional and volunteer youth workers in the church and in para-church ministries such as Young Life, Campus Life, and Fellowship of Christian Athletes work hard at building relationships with teenagers, modeling values, teaching skills, and pointing to Christ. We should look for ways to surround our kids with caring adults. And we should be that kind of caring and affirming adult for other teens.

Teenagers are expanding their relationships and finding close friendships outside the home. Let's guide them in the right direction in this important area of life.

Let's Party!

Parties are a vital part of teen life—for socializing, relaxation, fun, and entertainment. But a poorly planned party—or one without parental supervision—can have unwanted, even tragic consequences. Below are some suggestions to help you guide your teenager's party-going and party-hosting experiences.

WHEN YOUR TEENAGER IS ATTENDING A PARTY

1. Know where your teenager will be.
    - Get the address and phone number of the party giver.
    - Make sure your teen understands that you expect a phone call if the location changes.
2. Contact the parents of the party giver to . . .
    - verify the occasion.
    - offer assistance.
    - make sure a parent will be present at the party.
    - be certain that alcohol and other drugs will not be permitted.
3. Know how your teen will get to and from the party.
    - Assure your teen that you or a specific friend or neighbor can be called for a ride home.
    - Agree with your teenager that he or she will not ride in a car with a driver who has been drinking, or if driving himself or herself, will not drive under the influence.
    - You might make a "no questions asked" pact with your teen to call home.
4. Agree with your teenager on a time to come home.

- Be awake or have your teen awaken you when he or she arrives home.
- Make sure your teen knows to call if he or she is unable to come home on time.
- Agree on what will happen (consequences) if he or she doesn't come home on time.

5. If your teenager stays overnight with a friend after the party, check with the parents of the friend to verify that . . .
   - they want your teen to stay over.
   - they will be home.
   - you both agree on hours and other basic house rules.

6. You and your teenager may want to phone the party giver the next day to express your thanks.

WHEN YOUR TEENAGER IS HOSTING A PARTY

1. Set the ground rules with your teenager before the party.
   - Let your teen know what you expect.
   - Stress shared responsibility for hosting the party.
2. Be at home during the party.
   - Agree on an area of the house where the party will be held and where you can supervise adequately.
   - If you must be away, make sure another responsible adult is present. *Teenagers often host parties when parents are gone.* Agree with your teenager that this will never happen at your house.
3. Provide snacks and nonalcoholic beverages.
   - Sometimes you can ask guests to bring snacks to share.
   - If you have a punch bowl, supervise it. It is common for someone to add alcohol without your knowing it.
   - Avoid easy access to alcohol or other drugs in your home.
4. Notify your neighbors that there will be a party.

- This is especially important if loud music is involved.
- If neighbors are concerned, let them know that the party (or at least the noise) will end at a reasonable time (and agree with your teenager on that time).

5. Notify the police when hosting a large party.
   - This will help the police protect you and your neighbors.
   - If necessary, discuss with the police an agreeable plan for guest parking.

6. Limit party attendance and times.
   - Don't let the party get too big for you to handle. Small groups (under thirty) are best.
   - Have your teenager make a list of who's invited. *Do not allow party crashers.* Make sure everyone knows that up-front.
   - Set time limits for the party that enable teens to be home at a reasonable time.
   - Avoid open-house parties. It is difficult to control this type of party.

7. Don't allow guests to come and go.
   - This will discourage teens from leaving the party to drink alcohol or use drugs and then return.

8. Keep in mind that you may be taken to court on criminal charges or have to pay monetary damages in a civil lawsuit if you furnish alcohol or drugs to minors.
   - Be alert to the signs of alcohol or drug use.
   - Anyone who brings alcohol or drugs or refuses to cooperate with your rules should be asked to leave immediately. Be willing to call the police if unwanted guests refuse to leave the premises.
   - Notify parents of any teen who arrives at the party drunk or under the influence of drugs. *Do not let any teen drive under the influence of drugs or alcohol.*

9. Encourage your teenager to plan some activities or games.
   - Drinking and drug use are sometimes the result of boredom. Have fun activities planned in advance.
10. Supervise, don't smother.
   - Give the kids room to be themselves. Allow your teen to be alone with his or her friends but make yourself available. Just check on them from time to time.
   - Welcome your teenager's friends. Get to know them. Remember their names.
   - Don't get too upset or lose control if the kids mess up the house, break an expensive vase, or spill something on the carpet. It's better to expect damage and not get it than vice versa. Try to teen-proof your house ahead of time (put the expensive vase away). But take a deep breath, relax, and have fun. After all, it's a party!

THINK IT THROUGH

1. Can you remember the names of your close friends from your teenage years? What did you and your friends do together?
2. When did you first notice your children becoming obsessed with friends? What evidence did you see?
3. How have your teenagers' close friendships changed since elementary school? How do you feel about those changes?
4. Who are your kids' closest friends? How much time do they spend talking to each other on the phone every day? How often are they together each week?
5. Are the best friends good or bad influences on your teenagers? How do you know?

6. In what ways are your teenagers expressing their independence through their friendship choices? What clues to your teenagers' self-concept do you see through their circle of friends?

7. What can you do to support your church's youth ministry?

8. What steps can you take to get to know your teenagers' friends? How can you make your home a place where they will want to hang out?

9. How well do you know the parents of your teenagers' friends? What could you do to get to know them better? Why is this important for you to do?

10. When did you last have a positive, nonconfrontational discussion with your teenagers about friends and relationships? How did they respond? When would be the best time to do this?

11. What can you do to put your teens in contact with other caring adults—potential role models and mentors? What can you do to be that kind of person to other kids?

Teens Are Equipping Themselves for Adulthood

C huck threw back the covers, stepped out of bed, and walked to the window. As he pulled back the shade, sun streamed into the room. *Great!* he thought. *A beautiful Saturday and the perfect day to tackle my spring projects.*

A little later, sipping coffee at the breakfast table, Chuck scanned his list. "I guess I'll trim those limbs hanging over the garage roof first," he mused. "I should have taken care of that last fall. Then I'll work on the fence. I'll need to replace that rotting post and a few of the pickets. Then . . ." A few minutes later, Chuck eagerly walked outside, ready to tackle his projects.

Standing at the foot of the large tree, Chuck looked up at its branches. *Boy, they're longer than I remembered*, he thought.

After lugging out his extension ladder, leaning it against the garage, and climbing as high as he could and still see the branches, Chuck decided he needed a special tree limb saw to do the job right and to be safe. Unfortunately, he didn't have one, and, after making a few visits and calls, he determined that none of his neighbors had one either. So he put the ladder away and turned his attention to the next item on the list.

Chuck walked across the backyard to examine the post he wanted to replace, but he quickly realized that he would need to remove the other boards from the old post carefully, without breaking them. So he returned to the house and retrieved his claw hammer. After pulling the nails, he pushed and pulled on the post to loosen it and then tried to uproot it by hand. It wouldn't budge. So Chuck returned to the garage to find something to help him remove the post. He thought he would use a sledgehammer to loosen the post and a spade to dig it out. The first whack of the hammer, however, broke the post at ground level, where it was most rotten. Tossing the hammer aside, he picked up the spade and began digging. *This sure would be easier with a posthole digger*, he thought, *especially when I put in the new post.* And he thought about where he might obtain one. With such a small space in which to work, he certainly wasn't doing very well with the spade. After a few minutes of difficult digging but with no bottom of the old post in sight, he gave up and went inside.

TOOLS AND TOOLBOXES

Many of us have faced Chuck's dilemma and have learned by experience: *If you don't have the tools, you can't do the job!* Of course, you can make an attempt: Some have used paintbrushes and rolling pins when hanging wallpaper; some have used cookie sheets for snow removal; from time to time doctors have had to do surgery with pocketknives. But certainly the right tools make a dramatic difference in efficiency and job quality.

Actually, we need the right tools in every area of life—for learning, communicating, relating, and doing business. Also called "life skills," adults use them continually. One important task for adolescents is to equip themselves with the tools they will need when they are older.

It makes sense that these tools should be gathered during adolescence because, as we have already discussed, this is the time of the great transition from childhood to adulthood, and teens want to be seen and treated as autonomous adults. They need and *want* the tools.

These important tools fall into three broad categories.

The first is *responsibility*—knowing how to take charge of a task and get it done; learning to be reliable, dependable, and trustworthy.

Responsibility must be taught. Many people wonder why today's teenagers seem so irresponsible—as though responsibility should be inherited genetically. But responsibility is not a character trait or a talent that comes at birth; it is a skill that must be learned.

In the past, young people were more responsible than today's teenagers but only because they were given a good deal more responsibility than youth today. This happened not because parents were more enlightened than we are but out of necessity, for practical or economic reasons. If the children didn't pull their weight and help out, they likely wouldn't eat. In the natural order of life, this system provided a way for children to become capable, self-reliant adults.

In today's urban, technological society, child labor laws,

thankfully, protect children from abuse and exploitation. Many young people, however, have never had the opportunity to accept any meaningful responsibility. Parents, teachers, and other adults expect little from teenagers, and, as a result, teenagers receive very little experience in learning to become responsible adults. Sadly, some eighteen-year-olds haven't learned to wake themselves up and get going in the morning because they have never been given that responsibility.

"Responsibility" can be divided into two subcategories: responsibility for self and responsibility for things outside of oneself. Responsibility for self means having self-discipline; knowing how to delay gratification; understanding the difference between needs and wants; becoming a self-starter; learning restraint, self-control, and willpower; knowing how to "just say no."

According to Freud, maturity is the ability to postpone gratification. Babies, for example, can't wait for their needs to be met and will cry until the stomach is settled, the diaper is changed, or the bottle is given. Imagine an adult acting that way, throwing a tantrum in a restaurant because of slow service (hmm—maybe that's a bad example). In any case, adults are expected to be able to wait, exercise restraint, and meet their needs *at the appropriate time*. Obviously our teens waver between those two extremes, at times showing great patience but at other times acting like young children. During these years of transition, we need to teach teenagers to be self-disciplined.

Closely related is understanding the difference between needs and wants. Children may *want* candy, but they *need* sustenance. A child may *want* the toy advertised between Saturday morning cartoons, but she doesn't really *need* it. A junior higher may *want* the latest clothing fad, but he *needs* a warm coat.

The person who is self-disciplined says, "I am not a victim, and I can take responsibility for myself and for what happens to me."

Responsibility for things outside of oneself include following through on assignments, taking care of important matters, and being conscientious about a pet, personal belongings, or a job that needs to be done.

The second category of tools involves *interpersonal skills*—knowing how to express oneself and how to listen; knowing how to negotiate and compromise and how to handle frustration and anger.

It is very important for teenagers to learn how to interact successfully with others. If young people fail to learn good social skills, they will find themselves ill-equipped to function properly in a job or any kind of personal relationship. Some of the most important interpersonal skills that teenagers need to learn include:

- *Communicating*—the ability to exchange ideas with other people. Teenagers tend to communicate with one another in a kind of code language, using slang that is indecipherable to most adults. Because they have little experience communicating with adults, teens often result to shrugs, grunts, and an occasional "I dunno." Researchers in the business field have found that the people who are most likely to rise to the highest levels of their professions—regardless of the profession—are those who communicate well with others.

- *Listening and empathizing*—the ability to understand what others are saying and to see things from their point of view. This involves focusing on the other person during a conversation and conveying an understanding of that person's feelings and needs.

- *Cooperating*—the ability to work together with others toward a common goal.
- *Negotiating*—the ability to resolve conflict in a process of give-and-take. Unfortunately, children today learn conflict resolution from their superheroes, video games, TV shows, and society in general. And the message seems to be: Carry a gun and use it if necessary.
- *Sharing*—the ability to include other people in one's plans, experiences, and activities. Sharing includes aspects of humility and consideration for others. Not only is this beneficial, but it is also scriptural.

What's Wrong with This Picture?

I'm paid to be a foreman.
My job is leading men.
My boss thinks I'm a natural,
But if I am, why then—
I wish someone would tell me,
Why snow-swept walks I clean,
When in the house sit two grown sons
Who made the football team.

The third tool set is *good judgment*—knowing how to make an informed decision in this multiple-choice world; learning how to choose the best over everything else, even the "good"; knowing how to define, analyze, and resolve problems.

Kids are faced with more choices today than ever before, yet many of them have no real basis for making *good* choices. Instead, they make decisions based on factors such as:

- *Appearances.* This was the cause of the first sin recorded in the Bible. Eve "saw that the fruit of the tree was good for food and pleasing to the eye . . ." (Gen. 3:6), and she went for it. It never occurred to Eve to think through the long-term consequences of her decision (still being felt today!). Sadly, little has changed. Many teenagers (and adults) are encouraged to make decisions solely on how something looks or how cool it is. Ninety percent of all advertising is based on this principle. People buy automobiles and clothing and even choose mates based on appearance, not on whether the choice is a good one.

- *Feelings.* Our culture often determines rightness and wrongness not on absolute truth, but on feelings. "If it feels good, do it" is a principle that became popular in the 1960s and today is almost considered gospel. But as the Bible says, "There is a path before each person that seems right, but it ends in death" (Prov. 16:25 NLT).

- *Conformity.* Many teenagers won't do anything unless the crowd is doing it. Teens have a great desire to fit in and to be accepted, making conformity to the whims of the peer group a natural result. But doing what the crowd does is no basis for making wise decisions. Pontius Pilate, for example, made his decision to crucify Jesus based not on the facts but on what the crowd wanted (see Matt. 27:11–26).

Parents can help teenagers learn how to make good decisions based on what is right, what is true, and what is best for themselves and others. As Christian parents, we also want our children to learn to make decisions that are consistent with the Word of God. If they don't learn to do this while they are teenagers, their likelihood of ever learning it is very remote.

Remember, *if you don't have the tools, you can't do the job!*

MODEL VALUES AND TEACH SKILLS

In previous generations, children learned many of these life skills naturally because they had jobs to do—on the farm, in the family business, in the home, and through apprenticeships. This is no longer the case. According to Susan Littwin in *The Postponed Generation*, "It now takes ten years longer for people to become adults than it did just a generation ago. We now have thirty-year-old teenagers running around."[1] In most homes today, therefore, parents must be intentional in teaching important life skills, or the skills won't be passed on. We need to give teenagers the tools they will need later in life; we need to help them fill their toolboxes.

Life skills must be taught. We can't assume that children will learn them just by watching us. Certainly they catch a lot from our example, mostly in the area of values. We vividly illustrate what we value by how we invest our emotions, time, and money (this is discussed further in chapter 6). In fact, we cannot *not* model values. But skills must be taught.

Remember when you learned how to tie your shoes? Someone actually walked you through the process. All you learned by merely watching others was that tying shoes was important (a value reinforced from time to time when you tripped over your shoelaces). Eventually, someone explained, demonstrated, and guided you through the steps, and soon you were tying the laces by yourself. You have probably subsequently passed this skill on to your own children.

So the question before us is clear: How are we teaching our teenagers vital life skills? How are we equipping them with the right tools?

WHAT TO DO

In considering possible responses to this dilemma, we will reflect on each of the "tool sets" described above.

Training

By the age of eighteen, all children—male and female—should be familiar with and practiced at every aspect of running a home. They should be able to wash and iron their own clothes, prepare basic meals, run a vacuum cleaner, disinfect a bathroom, replace furnace filters, mow grass, weed garden areas, and so on. They should also be responsible for earning a portion of their spending money and budgeting it sensibly. This training not only helps prepare children for adulthood, it also develops in them an appreciation for the effort their parents put into maintaining a household, an effort children might otherwise take for granted.

John Rosemond, *John Rosemond's Six-Point Plan for Raising Happy, Healthy Children* (Kansas City, MO: Andrews and McMeel, 1989), 82.

Teach Responsibility

If we want our teenagers to become responsible, we need to give them the chance. This means:

Assigning important tasks and then allowing kids to succeed or fail. If we do everything for our kids and have low expectations for their performance, they most certainly will meet them. And they won't gain this important tool for their toolbox.

Instead, we can give our teenagers important tasks or jobs to perform within the family structure; we should assign chores and expect our kids to do them—well. Of course, these chores should match the individual child's age and maturity. The goal is to give children opportunities to make significant contributions to the family and to their world. In addition to teaching them how to handle responsibility, we want them to feel needed.

If you don't like the word *chores,* try calling these assignments "responsibilities." One family called them "contributions," and another used the euphemism "community service." Use whatever works for you.

Chores can be valuable because . . .

- they *endow kids with responsibility* and teach them some important skills they will need later in life.
- they *give kids the opportunity to do something important,* to contribute to the family, to feel needed. This, of course, builds self-esteem and self-worth in the best way possible. Kids may continue to grumble because they have to do chores, but if the chores they are doing are necessary and appreciated by the rest of the family (as opposed to busywork that nobody cares about), they will want to do them anyway. Chores allow kids to participate in the family, to be active players with important roles rather than passive benchwarmers. Such participation helps kids feel

more attached to the family and, therefore, more loyal to it and its values.

- they *teach kids the principle "Give, and it will be given to you" (Luke 6:38)*. Not only is this a biblical principle, but it is also good citizenship. In real life—whether regarding a job, family, church, marriage, or other relationship—those who get the most are those who give the most. That's how the world works. A person who is a contributor to society will have the best chance to enjoy its benefits. Free lunches are only available in welfare lines. Children who grow up without learning this principle at home more than likely will become extremely self-centered and unmotivated and will believe that they can have whatever they want for nothing.

Making Chores Work for Your Family—Twelve Tips

1. Assign chores to everyone in the family, including parents.
2. Make sure that everyone knows exactly what his or her chore is and when and how it is to be done. Be specific and reasonable.
3. Don't use chores as punishment.
4. Make the chores age-appropriate. Younger children can pick up their toys; older children can do laundry, maintain the lawn, and so on.
5. Allow kids some say in which chores they are responsible for. You could make a game of it. Perhaps have a drawing once a month to determine who gets to do particular chores.
6. Do some chores together as a family. Some projects are easier done as a group.

7. Give each person his or her own chores rather than assigning shared chores. This will reduce finger pointing and blaming when the chore isn't done.

8. Provide choices. For example: "Greg, we have company coming over Saturday afternoon. Do you plan to mow the lawn today or Saturday morning?" The choice is not *whether* Greg will mow the lawn, but *when*.

9. Create a family "chore chart." Such a chart can serve as a reminder as well as a way to monitor progress.

10. Don't expect perfection. Resist the temptation to "fix" a finished chore even though you know you can do a better job.

11. Always show appreciation when a chore has been completed. Everyone likes to know that his or her efforts have not gone unnoticed.

12. Give kids feedback they can use the next time. Don't just criticize inadequately done jobs but offer suggestions and help for doing a better job in the future.

As a meaningful chore, a sixth grader could be expected to care for a favorite pet. This responsibility would involve buying the food, making appointments with the veterinarian, and so forth. A sixteen-year-old could be given the responsibility of using the Internet to research the best airline prices for the family vacation, presenting the findings at a family meeting, and then purchasing the tickets. Another teen could help plan and prepare the family meals. In each of these assignments, the parents should give feedback, hold the young person accountable for completing the assignment, and reward a job well done.

Attaching consequences to behaviors and enforcing them consistently. We will cover this in more detail in chapter 11, but for now suffice it to say that unless our children are allowed to experience the consequences of their actions, they will never learn to be responsible.

Chores and Allowances

Should you pay kids to do chores? Should their allowances be tied to responsibilities around the house? Here are some general guidelines:

1. It is better to give each child an allowance (a portion of the family income) separate from chores.

2. Chores should be each person's responsibility to the family, regardless of whether they are paid for doing them. If chores are tied to income, then when the child doesn't need the money, he or she simply won't do the chore.

3. You can, however, allow kids to earn extra money by doing extra work. This work should be something that you probably would pay someone else to do. For example, if you are in the habit of getting your car washed at the local car wash, you could offer your teenager the chance to earn that money.

4. Rather than connecting chores with money, connect them with consequences. Privileges usually come with responsibilities. If your teenager doesn't want the responsibility, then he or she will be faced with giving up a corresponding privilege.

5. Help your teenager learn to manage money properly by increasing his or her allowance over time and by giving him or her increased responsibility for personal expenses, such as clothing, eating out, extracurricular activities, gasoline, dating, entertainment, car insurance, and so forth.

Emphasizing self-discipline. We can teach this valuable life skill by explaining the importance of setting priorities and then showing kids how to make "to do" lists and how to prioritize daily. We can give them calendars and explain how to schedule their time. We can explain the purpose of a budget, show them ours, and then help them set up their own.

In this regard, many parents make the mistake of saying, "We can't afford it" when pressured by children to make a big purchase. This statement implies that the family *does not have enough money.* In reality, the decision to buy or to not buy something is usually determined by a values choice, not by cost. For example, one father explained to his son, "Yes, we could buy that car"—the latest model luxury car, fully loaded—"but you wouldn't be able to go to college." In other words, the parents did not decide not to buy the car because they couldn't get the money together but because they had chosen to spend it (in this case save it to spend later) elsewhere. Another mom and dad explained to their children, "We're glad the Carlsons are taking a vacation in Europe this summer. We could, too, but we wouldn't be able to eat for a year." (Again, they were saying that technically they could "afford" the European vacation, but it would take quite a sacrifice.) These parents then suggested that the family work together on a plan for saving money for a year or two so that, eventually, they could travel to an exotic locale.

Some parents allow their teens to have their own checking accounts and then provide them with enough income to reasonably cover all their living expenses, excluding room and board. The teenager has to budget money for clothes, school supplies, lunch, entertainment, and all nonessentials. Once teenagers learn how a budget works, they will understand the value of buying less-expensive shoes in order to have money left for other purchases. Some teenagers become pretty good bargain hunters and start shopping in thrift stores in order to save money for a summer trip or a car.

Another idea is to encourage teenagers to save money in mutual funds or to begin investing in the stock market. The purpose is not to push teens into the world of high finance but to help them develop a sense of responsibility, self-discipline, and good judgment.

We'll discuss this further in chapter 11.

Helping the teenager find a niche. This means helping young people discover what they are good at and then encouraging them to do it. What do your teenagers like to do? What are their natural talents and abilities? How have they been gifted? Many teenagers will try to establish their unique identities by pursuing and often excelling in a hobby or special interest, such as playing the guitar, drawing cartoons, or raising pigs. Some "taggers" (graffiti artists) are actually very talented kids who just need a positive way to express themselves rather than engaging in vandalism. Quite often, the interest that a teenager shows in a particular field (sports, computers, music, drama, cars, writing) can lead to a career in a related field. Remember the fighter pilots during Operation Desert Storm? They grew up playing video games. Don't be discouraged if your teenager is pursuing activities that seem pointless to you right now. The teenager who spends hours surfing or reading murder mysteries may find a career in oceanography or law enforcement.

Also, aptitude and "patterning" tests can help determine a person's interests and competencies. We can use one of those tests. In addition, we can encourage our teenagers to seek the counsel of other adults who know them well. The main thing is to help teenagers follow their hearts and develop the skills that come naturally and easily.

Allowing teens to find good jobs. Many parents wonder whether their teenagers should be allowed (or encouraged) to get jobs. According to government statistics, more than one-third of all teenagers today have part-time jobs, working as many as twenty hours per week. Eleven percent hold down full-time jobs. But are teen jobs necessary or beneficial?

In most cases, they are not. Most teen jobs today are demeaning and monotonous, a source of cheap labor for employers and nothing more than a source of spending money for teens. Rarely do kids actually need the money for essentials. But today's materialistic culture leads them to believe that they need a job in order to get money in order to buy stuff. Today's teenagers suffer from what has been called "premature affluence," the ability to finance consumer binges even as their parents are cutting back. In addition, teens with jobs tend to experience more stress, have less free time to participate in extracurricular activities, and have lower grades.

Summer employment or a weekend job that provides a healthy working and learning environment can be a good experience for a teenager. Today, most people judge a job as "good" by the amount of pay that's involved. For teenagers, however, a good job provides mentoring by an adult supervisor, the chance to learn new job-related skills, and a sense of having accomplished something worthwhile. Good jobs can benefit kids who are willing to work and want to be more responsible and self-reliant. They can also help teenagers to feel valued, as though they are contributing to society. We should allow teenagers to find good jobs. But if they want jobs simply so they can have more discretionary income to satisfy their materialistic urges, they should be discouraged or prohibited.

Sharing what we know. Parents each have thirty or more years of experience from which kids can learn. We should look for ways to pass on the wisdom and lessons that we have learned over our lifetimes. Sometimes this means explaining to teenagers why we do what we do. They may not act as though they are listening, but they will pick up more than we think. The key is not to preach at them or lecture them, but to share our thoughts and ideas in an atmosphere of friendliness, respect, and support.

Modeling responsible behavior. Like it or not, our children probably will grow up to be very similar to us. So we must be good examples of what we expect of our kids. This includes how we prioritize and discipline ourselves, how we shop and spend money, and how we fulfill our responsibilities and keep our commitments . . . on time. It also includes modeling our important values and the role of faith in our lives. As children become teenagers, they start watching parents with a more critical eye, and they take their cues from Mom and Dad. "If my parents can be irresponsible and get away with it," they reason, "so can I." On the other hand, teens who watch their parents take on responsibility, make good choices, and delay gratification for a higher good will learn to appreciate the value of being a responsible person.

Teach Interpersonal Skills

Because teenagers are so focused on relationships and concerned about friends, we will have many opportunities to teach interpersonal skills, especially those related to communication. To do this, we can:

Listen to our kids more. One big reason that kids don't feel comfortable talking with adults is because few adults take the time to listen to them. If no one is listening, why talk? Teens have coined their own language for communicating among themselves, but they have little experience talking with adults.

We can teach good interpersonal skills by being better listeners. If we practice active listening, our kids will open up. They may even look forward to having conversations with us.

Listening is the best way to show respect. When we listen to someone, we communicate to that person: *Your thoughts and ideas have value to me. I am interested in what you have to say.* This, by the way, is the best way to teach kids about prayer. Many teenagers struggle with prayer because they find it hard to believe that God, the Creator of the universe, would listen to them. The reason they find this tough to believe is because their own parents don't listen. The value of listening goes way beyond getting information. It is the language of love. We'll discuss this further in chapters 7 and 8.

Encourage dialogue in the family. We should work at having good conversation among family members and others. This can begin around the dinner table perhaps, and then move to the family room or other places. Warning: It probably will necessitate turning off the TV and, in the car, turning down the radio. If everyone seems too busy for impromptu, unplanned conversations, we can be more intentional by planning family meetings on a regular basis during which family members can share what's going on in their lives. During these meetings, we can make plans for the week, discuss coming events (like the summer vacation), and so on. Family meetings don't have to be long; just doing them is important. They give kids a chance to be heard and encourage them to express their opinions and ideas in a supportive atmosphere. Family meetings can provide a positive forum for dialogue. And these meetings should be fun, not just the time when parents remind everyone of the rules or share information. We shouldn't take ourselves too seriously.

Look for opportunities to instruct. Perhaps the best time to

teach a communication skill is after a communication breakdown. Let's say, for example, that your daughter misunderstood
an important English assignment. You could explain the importance of writing down each assignment when it is given in class
and then double-checking to make sure it was understood.

> When kids observe conflict between parents, it can be a great
> learning experience for them to witness the conflict resolution
> too.
>
> —Kendra Smiley

It is important for us to reinforce good communication
skills by example. Unfortunately, this is often where the
process goes awry as we blame our teenagers for every communication breakdown and misunderstanding. Instead, we
should double-check to make sure that our message has been
heard and understood.

In the Campus Life/JV materials (a life skills–based curriculum), early adolescents are taught to GTE if they want to "get
what they need." G stands for "Go into the same room." That
is, if someone wants to communicate with another person, it
helps if they are in the same room and not shouting up the stairs
and through closed doors. T stands for "Turn toward the person" and emphasizes the importance of face-to-face communication. This seems obvious, but think of how many times you
have struggled to hear what someone was saying while he or she
was turned away from you. Finally, E stands for "Eye contact"—looking the person in the eye when you talk. Again, this
seems obvious to us as adults, but it's difficult for teenagers
who tend to mumble with their heads bowed.

A simple lesson like GTE could be taught and acted out at a family meeting. Remember, however, that you should be accountable for "GTE-ing" too. So when you're tempted to yell, "Dinner's ready!"—don't. Instead, walk up the stairs, knock on your teenager's door, **G**o into the room, **T**urn toward your teen, look him or her in the **E**ye, and say, "Dinner's ready." What a good example you will be!

Play games together as a family. Playing games can pull a family together and build lasting memories. And many interpersonal skills can be taught and modeled in game playing (for example, negotiating, compromising, playing fair, being a good winner or loser, dealing with frustration, working as a team, and so forth). Some games such as Taboo, Pictionary, Boggle, The UnGame, and Password also involve good communication and interaction.

Avoid communication busters. Sometimes we discourage dialogue by interrupting our teenagers when they want to ask a question or tell us something or by using terminal language. Words and phrases such as "Why can't you ever . . . ?"; "How come you never . . . ?"; "Surely you realize . . . ?"; "How many times do I have to tell you . . . ?"; "Why are you being so childish?"; "When will you ever grow up?"; "Did you . . . ?"; "Can you . . . ?"; "Will you . . . ?"; "Won't you . . . ?"; "Are you . . . ?"; "Aren't you . . . ?" will shut down communication faster than we can say, "I told you so!"

Ask questions that encourage dialogue. Too often the communication between parent and teen is one-way, from the parent to the teen. Instead, we need to work at *dialogue,* having a good two-way discussion or conversation with the young person.

The bottom line: We reinforce and model good communication skills by the way we interact with our kids. They learn from us.

CLASP

To resolve most conflicts, just remember to CLASP.

C means "Calm down." When you are attacked verbally—someone is angry with you or is trying to start an argument—don't say anything right away . . . calm down.

L means "Lower your voice." In other words, *do not yell*—speak in a lower, gentle voice when you answer.

A means "Acknowledge his or her request." This is especially important when someone wants you to do something that you don't want to do. Let's say your mother tells you to go to the store, but you want to finish reading your book. You would calm down, speak softly, and say something like, "You want me to go to the store. What would you like me to get?"

S means "State your request." This is explaining your side—what you would like to do. In our previous example, you could say, "I really would like to finish this book first, if that's all right. I'm right near the end."

P means "Propose a solution." In other words, suggest a way that will resolve the issue where you both can be happy or satisfied. Again, using our previous example, you could then say, "Would it be all right if I at least finished this page? Then I'll go to the store and get everything on your list."

"How to Be a Better Family Member," meeting #5, from *Campus Life/JV, Year One* (Wheaton, IL: Youth for Christ/USA, 1987).

Teach Good Judgment

A strong case can be made that good judgment is the most important tool. With so many values, life styles, philosophies, and theology options assaulting young people from every direction, they can easily become overwhelmed and confused. Certainly many teenagers make the wrong decisions, the wrong choices. To teach good judgment, we can:

Trust our teenagers with more of their own decisions. Unless the consequences are far too serious to allow this, we should begin letting our teenagers learn to choose wisely by personal experience. We need to resist the temptation to rescue our teens by making important decisions for them, even though it may seem easier and safer. We can set limits to prevent dangerous or immoral behavior, but our goal should be to help our teens develop good judgment.

Judgmental Skills

Judgmental skills develop when parents, teachers, and other adults create or allow children to become involved in situations from which they cannot escape except through thinking.

H. Stephen Glenn and Jane Nelson, *Raising Self-Reliant Children in a Self-Indulgent World* (Rocklin, CA: Prima Publishing, 1989), 198.

Teach our teenagers to make good decisions. Most decisions are very complicated, so we need to give our children the tools they will need to sort through all of the issues. We can do this by giving them a framework for making decisions.

For example, we might help them think through their options and possibilities. Begin by listing all the possible courses of action. Next, evaluate each option based on possible outcomes and consequences, asking, "What will happen if I choose this option or that one?"

Teenagers can be taught to make decisions with specific goals in mind. And they can be taught to think through the long-term consequences of their decisions.

Sometimes just showing a teenager how to make a list of pros and cons can be very helpful. (Draw a line down the middle of the page, and start listing the pros on one side, and the cons on the other. Give each item a value, say 1 through 10, to indicate their relative importance. Add them up to see which column outweighs the other.)

While such methods are very limited in their actual usefulness, they do help young people think through their decisions, sort out the issues, differentiate between wants and needs or reality and wishful thinking. Once kids have a framework for making good decisions, they will be more likely to make them.

Avoid panicking when our teenagers make bad decisions. Sometimes the best lessons are learned by making mistakes. We shouldn't rescue our kids all the time. We will discuss this further in chapter 11.

Affirm good decisions and process bad ones. After the fact, we can review what happened in the decision-making process.

In their book *Raising Self-Reliant Children in a Self-Indulgent World*, H. Stephen Glenn and Jane Nelson suggest the What? Why? How? process. When a teenager makes a bad choice, rather than lecturing or scolding, the parent should ask three questions: What happened? Why do you think it happened? and How can we learn from what happened? or How can you do it differently next time to get a different result? Asking what, why, and how questions such as these in a respectful and supportive way can help teenagers learn from their mistakes and become more responsible. We need to be careful here, however. Questions such as What in the world were you thinking? Why would you do such a thing? or How could you have been so stupid? communicate hostility and disrespect, and they don't lend themselves to learning and growth.

Involve our teenagers in the decisions we make. For example, you might take your teenager with you the next time you go shopping for a new car, for new furniture, or even for groceries.

Family meetings can be good forums for processing relatively small decisions, such as what the family should do this Christmas (stay home or go to Grandma's house?), or big decisions, such as whether Dad should take a new, higher-paying job (which may require longer hours or moving to another state). Kids need to know what goes into such decisions. Ultimately, we must make these decisions, but teenagers can benefit from knowing why we choose the way we do.

Whenever making a decision, it is wise to think out loud and ask our teenagers' opinions. The only way our kids can learn from our experience is if we share it with them.

Teach teenagers to seek God's will. For Christians, an important consideration in making decisions is God's will: Is my decision consistent with what God would want me to do? Of course, the best place to find God's will is in the Bible. Not every decision or problem is addressed directly in Scripture (no R-rated movies premiered in Nazareth when Jesus was a teenager), but teens can be taught to look for principles and guidelines that will inform their decisions. Again, rather than condemning our kids for every bad choice they make, we should help them learn from their mistakes and seek guidance from God's Word.

In recent years, tens of thousands of teenagers have become familiar with the four letters "WWJD," which stand for "What

Would Jesus Do?" This campaign, with its accompanying bracelets, T-shirts, hats, books, and other paraphernalia, attempts to sensitize people to an important decision-making principle: As followers of Christ, we need to make sure that all our decisions are based on the teachings and modeling of Jesus Christ.

Right Decisions

A young man was appointed to the presidency of a large bank at the tender age of thirty-two. The promotion was far beyond his wildest dreams and rather frightening to him, so he went to the venerable old chairman of the board to ask for advice.

"What is the most important thing for me to do as a new president?" he asked the older man.

"Right decision," was the gentleman's terse answer.

The young man thought for a moment and said, "Thank you very much; that is very helpful. But can you be a bit more specific? How do I make right decisions?"

The wise old man answered, "Experience."

Exasperated, the young president said, "But that is why I'm here. I don't have the experience I need to make right decisions. How do I get experience?"

"Wrong decisions," came the old man's reply.

Ben Patterson, *Waiting: Finding Hope When God Seems Silent* (Downers Grove, IL: InterVarsity Press, 1991), 162.

Teenagers who are seeking autonomy may not want their parents making their decisions for them anymore, but they still want guidance and direction. For many Christian teenagers, the Bible, the church, the youth minister, a trusted counselor, or a Christian book can provide them with the guidance and authority they seek. Thus, we should encourage our kids to take advantage of those resources. We can also encourage our teenagers to pray, asking God for wisdom and guidance when making important decisions. Again, if we model this behavior in front of our kids, they will learn that this is how adult Christians make good choices.

Teens are equipping themselves for adulthood, and we can help them find the right tools: responsibility, interpersonal relationships, and good judgment. Remember, if you don't have the tools, you can't do the job!

Measure of Discipline
Also Measure of Love

"You don't love me!" How many times have your kids laid that one on you? And how many times have you, as a parent, resisted the urge to tell them how much? Some day, when my children are old enough to understand the logic that motivates a mother, I'll tell them.

I loved you enough to bug you about where you were going, with whom, and what time you would get home.

I loved you enough to insist you buy a bike with your own money that you could afford.

I loved you enough to be silent and let you discover your friend was a creep.

I loved you enough to make you return a Milky Way with a bite out of it to a drugstore and confess, "I stole this."

I loved you enough to stand over you for two hours while you cleaned your bedroom, a job that would have taken me fifteen minutes.

I loved you enough to say, "Yes, you can go to Disney World on Mother's Day."

I loved you enough to let you see anger, disappointment, disgust, and tears in my eyes.

I loved you enough not to make excuses for your lack of respect or your bad manners.

I loved you enough to admit that I was wrong and ask for your forgiveness.I loved you enough to ignore what every other mother did or said.

I loved you enough to let you stumble, fall, hurt, and fail.

I loved you enough to let you assume the responsibility for your own actions at age six, ten, or sixteen.

I loved you enough to figure you would lie about the party being chaperoned, but I forgave you for it—after discovering I was right.

I loved you enough to accept you for what you are, not for what I wanted you to be.

But most of all, I loved you enough to say no when you hated me for it. That was the hardest part of all.

Erma Bombeck, Universal Press Syndicate, 1986.

THINK IT THROUGH

1. Recently, on what project did you have to suspend work because you didn't have the right tools?
2. During your adolescence, what skills did you learn that

have proved to be invaluable to you as an adult? How did you learn those skills?

3. What were some of your chores growing up? Which of these chores did you dislike the most? Why? Which chore taught you the most?

4. What values do you think you are modeling for your children? What life skills have you tried to teach them?

5. What evidence of *irresponsibility* do you see in your teenager? What evidence of *responsibility* do you see?

6. How can you and your spouse help your teenagers become self-disciplined?

7. How are your teenagers learning to manage money?

8. What can you do to help your teenagers find their niches?

9. What caused the most recent interpersonal conflict in your home? How was that conflict resolved?

10. When have your children seen you negotiate? Compromise?

11. When did you last have a family meeting? What did you discuss? How can you make your family meetings more interesting and fun?

12. What big family decision needs to be made? What can you do to involve your teenagers in making that decision?

13. How does your relationship with God affect your decision-making process?

Chapter 6

Teens Are Developing Personal Values and Beliefs

- From all outward appearances, Nate was the ideal Christian. His family had always been very active in church, with his parents holding several leadership positions through the years. You could always count on Nate and his family—if the church was open, they were there! As a young boy, Nate had won the annual Sunday school Scripture memory contests, and every summer he had attended Vacation Bible School and youth camp. Nate's church involvement continued and even increased during his adolescent years, culminating in his being elected state president of the denomination's youth ministry. *What a solid Christian and such a good example,* church members thought. So you can imagine the shock when, after Nate's sophomore year at the state university, he announced to his family that he had become an atheist.

• Always an excellent student, Shaleen enjoyed reading and thinking things through. And although the attention of many of her friends had turned to sports, boys, or parties in junior high and high school, Shaleen had continued to focus on her education, taking accelerated courses and doing quite well. While pleased with Shaleen's grades, her parents wondered where she had picked up her skeptical bent—Shaleen seemed to question everything the teachers and other authorities said. In fact, last week in Sunday school, Shaleen had caused quite a stir when she admitted to having serious doubts about her faith. "Sometimes I even wonder if God exists," she had said. But Shaleen didn't say much more after the teacher had explained that "doubt is the opposite of faith" and that "Christians shouldn't doubt."

• Tired of the suburban rut and of always being the "good kid," Grant emptied his bank account and ran away to the city to find his fame and fortune. For a while Grant had no problem landing part-time jobs that paid well; after all, he was young, strong, and good-looking. It felt great to be on his own, away from the confinements of home, church, and neighborhood. Grant had plenty of money and friends and could live as he pleased—every night was a party. Although Grant was living beyond his means, he hardly noticed because he was having so much fun . . . until his landlord evicted him for not paying his rent. That began Grant's downward spiral as he lost his job, his friends, and eventually his health. Finally, desperate, he decided to swallow his pride and head back to where he knew he would get a decent meal and a bed—home. Grant felt tremendous guilt about hurting his family and shame for what he had done, but he started hitchhiking the long miles back. Several hours later, he was almost there. Then with a muttered, "Thanks for the ride," Grant emerged from the car and stood at the end of the familiar winding driveway. Slowly he shuffled toward the house. But suddenly he was aware of someone running toward him and shouting his name: "Grant, Grant! My son, my son! You've come home!" and he fell into the embrace of his father.

Perhaps Nate, Shaleen, and Grant sound like teenagers in your life, maybe even in your home. Although these stories are quite different, they share a common theme: developing personal values and beliefs. Let's take a closer look at each individual.

Nate is an environmental Christian. That is, he grew up surrounded by Christianity: a strong Christian home, a solid Christian church, and numerous good Christian friends and activities. On the outside, during Nate's adolescence, everything looked great, spiritually and otherwise. Even beneath the surface, Nate felt fine, not harboring any dark habits or secret doubts about God, Jesus, or the Bible. In fact, he could give a fine and very sincere testimony and often won quizzes on Bible knowledge. But Nate's "faith" was not his own; instead, he was merely reflecting what his parents, pastor, and other church leaders believed. So when Nate left the environment, he left the faith.

Shaleen is trying to make her faith her own. She is meeting resistance, however, because the Christian adults in her life want teenagers to repeat the church's beliefs instead of questioning them. But Shaleen has learned how to think; thus, she is looking for the truth. Shaleen doesn't accept statements any more just because someone in authority makes them or because they have been repeated often. She wants to know why and to see the evidence. Shaleen is a good kid with high moral standards, and she certainly doesn't see herself as a rebel. But her Sunday school teacher's response upset her, and she's not sure that she wants to go back to class.

Grant's story probably sounded very familiar since it echoes the experience of a young man in one of Jesus' parables. Jesus had told his story for the benefit of the gathered crowds, especially the religious leaders (Luke 15:11–32). We know nothing about Grant's faith, but it is clear that he wanted to leave the values of his family and community and strike out on his own. Eventually, when Grant came to his senses and returned, his father welcomed him with open arms. In Jesus' story, the older brother who had faithfully remained at home and had *not* rejected his father's values and beliefs became incensed at this turn of events; after all, his younger brother had turned his back on the family, had blown all his money, and had lived immorally. Now that this younger brother was repentant, he deserved *something*, but not a warm welcome and certainly not a party! (It's easy to identify with the older brother's feelings and actions, isn't it?)

We could highlight several other case studies of this adolescent values struggle. Perhaps it is occurring right now in your home or in a family close to you. Whatever the outcome, each struggle touches everyone who knows and loves the young person involved.

SERIOUS THINKING

Teenagers, especially middle and older adolescents, are doing some serious thinking—about life, their values, and their faith.

They are trying to make sense of what they have seen and heard since they were children, and life has to make sense to them. This can be scary to our teens and threatening to us. But it needs to happen—it's part of their transition, their growing autonomy, and their emerging adulthood. Actually this push to develop personal values and beliefs should be good news to Christian adults—studies have revealed that 85 percent of those who profess faith in Christ do so when they are teenagers.

When they were very young, our children accepted most everything they were told, and they believed pretty much what we, their parents, believed. But they need belief systems of their own. So as they begin to think and reason and push to find their own identity, they want those belief systems *now*. What they come up with will probably be carried into adulthood.

GROWING PAINS

In chapter 2 we discussed the transition that takes place in adolescents from concrete to conceptual thinking. As adolescents begin to discover that they can think and reason for themselves, they can become very argumentative. Some teens question everything; they disagree just to disagree. Commenting on this characteristic, one parent said, "My eighth-grade daughter would make a great lawyer. She has strong opinions about everything and reasons to back up her opinions. Of course, this also means that she can rationalize just about anything she wants to do. Yeah, I can see her in a courtroom—she would do very well!"

Add this combativeness to the push for independence, and you can see why teens and parents tend to argue a lot. Our kids seem to question everything we say, just because *we* are saying it. Actually, teenagers will often accept a statement from another adult (youth leader, teacher, coach, pastor, friend, or neighbor) much more readily than from a parent, even if Mom or Dad says the same thing. The constant arguments can be frustrating for parents as they attempt to teach their adolescent children Bible concepts and other important truths and try to guide them through society's moral morass.

Default Creation

In the vacuum where traditional behavioral expectations for young people used to exist, in the silence of empty homes and neighborhoods, young people have built their own community. The adolescent community is a creation by default, an amorphous grouping of young people that constitutes the world in which adolescents spend their time. Their dependence on each other fulfills the universal human longing for community and inadvertently cements the notion of a tribe apart. More than a group of peers, it becomes in isolation a society with its own values, ethics, rules, worldview, rites of passage, worries, joys, and momentum. It becomes teacher, advisor, entertainer, challenger, nurturer, inspirer, and sometimes destroyer.

Patricia Hersch, *A Tribe Apart* (New York: Fawcett-Columbine, 1998), 21.

Speaking of morals and society, check out the contemporary cultural context in which our kids are developing their personal values and beliefs. It makes this process even more complex. In today's neutral-values society, teenagers find it increasingly difficult to get the truth about what is right or wrong, good or bad, true or false. Often they receive mixed messages from the older generation. For example, parents, teachers, and celebrities encourage young people to "Just say no!" to a variety of behaviors, including premarital sex. Yet the clear message modeled on just about every television sitcom and drama is "Just say yes," as characters move quickly through throwaway relationships and hop from bed to bed. Kids also see greedy professional athletes, supposedly role models, going only for the "gold" (as in millions) and engaged in every type of aberrant and illegal behavior. Or consider the morality modeled by our political leaders. As George Will and other pundits have poignantly noted, we have "dumbed down" our moral standards in America.

INFLUENCERS

With these pervasive mixed messages and negative role models, it may seem virtually impossible for teenagers to develop the right kind of values and beliefs, especially since conventional wisdom is that teenagers are primarily influenced by their peers and the media. But is this true? Are peers and the media the most powerful influencers of today's teenagers? Do they determine all values and beliefs?

According to researchers, the answer is no. Numerous studies have been conducted over the last few years to find out who or what influences teenagers the most, and the studies agree that parents remain the single most important influence, all the way through high school. A 1997 study, conducted by researchers at the University of Minnesota and the University of North Carolina, surveyed 12,000 students in grades 7 through 12; they found that the closer teenagers were to their parents, the less likely they were to smoke, use drugs, drink alcohol, engage in violence, commit suicide, or have sex at a young age. This study also found that a teenager's connection to schools and teachers played a significant role.[1] Another survey of 272,400 teenagers conducted by *USA Weekend* magazine found that 70 percent of teens identified their parents as the most important influence in their lives. Twenty-one percent said that about their friends (peers), and only 8 percent named the media (TV shows).[2]

In general, all the research on this subject produces this list of the primary influences on teenagers:

1. Parents
2. Extended family (grandparents, other relatives)
3. Adults outside the home (teachers, coaches, youth workers, a friend's parents, a boss)
4. Same age peers
5. The media (TV, movies, music)

Most people would create a similar list if they thought about it for a while. How many adults do you know who look back on their teen years and credit one of their peers as their most important influence? Have you ever heard an adult say, "I am what I am today thanks largely to the Doobie Brothers"? Probably not. True, some people became Deadheads or Trekkies or were otherwise heavily influenced by popular culture, *but they are in the minority*. News bulletins often feature kids who imitate the behavior of gangsta rappers or commit serious crimes after watching violent movies, but their numbers are very small compared to those who look first to their parents and other trusted adults for guidance.

This, of course, directly contradicts the common view that the peer group and the media are the most powerful influencers of teenagers. Why do so many people assume that to be true? Perhaps it is because, for a growing segment of the teen population, it *is* true. In today's world, more and more kids are growing up without positive adult connections. Parents are absent. The extended family is dead. And fewer teenagers have adults outside the home to mentor and encourage them. For these kids, the peer group and the media have become the primary influences on them *by default*. They are not the primary influences because they are inherently more powerful and alluring than parents and other adults, but because parents and other adults are less available. Remove parents, extended family, and other adults, and all kids have left is the peer group and the media to influence them.

This is important to remember. As caring adults, and especially as parents, we need to *be there* for our adolescents, even if they don't seem to want us around. And we need to provide our kids with adult mentors. If we can surround them with caring adults and positive role models, they will have a much better chance for success as they grow into adulthood. H. Stephen Glenn put it this way: "Every teenager, left to his own devices, will always gravitate to the oldest person he can find who will take him seriously and treat him with dignity and respect."[3] That's why kids are such hero worshipers. They are always looking for someone older and wiser to show them how to be and how to act.

Certainly teens are developing personal values and beliefs, sometimes aggressively. In this process, however, they need and want adults to guide them in the right direction.

> Example is not the main thing in influencing others . . . it's the only thing.
>
> —Albert Schweitzer

WHAT TO DO

First, *we should not panic* if our teenagers don't share our values and beliefs right now. Often kids temporarily reject the values of their parents in order to come up with their own. Like trapeze artists at the circus, kids let go of their childhood beliefs to fly through the air and grasp a new set. More often than not, this new set is very similar to the one left behind. Or they might swing back to the place they left. Proverbs 22:6 reminds us: "Teach your children to choose the right path, and when they are older, they will remain upon it" (NLT). We should trust the process.

Second, *we should not expect our teenagers to be spiritual giants* and to have all their belief systems in order. Teenagers who are put on spiritual pedestals usually fall. They are not mature enough to meet the expectations for someone in that role. Teens on pedestals often feel like phonies, or, like Nate at the beginning of this chapter, they crash and burn when they leave the Christian environment. Teenagers' faith, just like the other parts of their lives, is in transition.

Third, *we should avoid preaching.* In other words, we shouldn't try to force-feed our values and beliefs to our adolescents. Lectures aren't very effective with teenagers. Stan Beard says, "I used to talk to my kids a lot about God. Now I talk to God a lot about my kids."

Fourth, *we should discuss important issues* with our teenagers. We shouldn't assume that they're not interested or that they would be bored. Unfortunately, some parents avoid discussing theology, philosophy, ethics, politics, morality, and other similar topics because they fear being asked difficult questions. But it's all right to admit we don't know something

You Can't Give Away What You Don't Own

Just as you can't give away your neighbor's lawn mower, you can't pass on his values to your kids. They must be yours. Those values must be bought with a price, or they won't stand up against the political correctness of our day. Let's face reality. Believing in strong Christian ideals can cause a person to lose more friends than having bad breath. With all the talk about family values today, our kids have totally tuned those words out. If they aren't identified, talked about, and given as high a place of importance as your new golf clubs, you can forget about your teens having a desire to live them out.

Bill Sanders, *Seize the Moment, Not Your Teen* (Wheaton, IL: Tyndale, 1997), 70–71.

and to suggest looking for answers together. We need to find out what our teenagers think. In this regard, we should accept and even encourage our kids' doubts. It's good to doubt *if the doubter is looking for answers.*

Fifth, *we should be good listeners.* When teenagers begin to state their opinions, especially strong or controversial ones, parents often interrupt, anticipating where the line of reasoning is going and providing answers. Instead, we should focus on what the teenagers are saying, even physically leaning toward them to demonstrate with our body language that we are interested. And instead of interrupting or coming back with quick answers, we should reflect ("So you're saying that . . ."), clarify ("Do you mean . . ."), or empathize ("I know what you mean, . . ."). Active listening takes others seriously. It lets them know that we think they have something important to contribute. By listening to our teenagers, we will encourage them to share their thoughts and ideas with us.

An Example Is Worth a Thousand Words

(A few actions you can take that will
make a big impression on your kids)

Love God.

Love your kids.

Love your spouse.

Pray often.

Study Scripture regularly.

Go to church every week.

Worship with gusto when you go.

Read a lot of good books.

Volunteer to serve in a ministry of the church.

Listen to good music.

Turn off the TV.

Celebrate family traditions, birthdays, anniversaries, holidays, and special occasions.

Tithe regularly.

Support an underprivileged child through a Christian relief organization.

Participate in a service project as a family, such as helping to serve Thanksgiving dinner at a homeless shelter.

Be generous; share your stuff with others.

Practice hospitality; invite other families to your home for dinner.

Speak positively of other Christians.

Make integrity a priority.

Practice what you preach.

When you don't know, admit it.

Love your spouse.

Love your kids.

Love God.

(Add your own ideas!)

Sixth, *we should model the values* that we want our teenagers to learn. As we discussed in chapter 5, we need to model values and teach skills. This means living the values that we want our kids to catch. So we should let them know what makes us tick, what controls our lives. This includes being open, honest, and vulnerable. It may not seem as though our teenagers are listening to us, but they sure are watching us.

Seventh, and finally, *we should support the church's youth ministry.* Positive peer pressure can reinforce the values we model and teach in our homes. And teenagers will be more likely to take a stand for Christ if they can do it with others. At a recent True Love Waits rally, more than fifteen thousand teenagers marched forward to commit themselves to sexual abstinence until marriage. It is very unlikely that many of those kids would have been able to make such a stand alone.

Living Values

Parents cannot teach values without living them. Those who perpetually sacrifice family time for work—missing children's school events, pretending a business trip is a family vacation—send a clear message that acquisition and self-gratification are more important than commitment and loving relationships.

Our obligations to our children cannot be fulfilled by sending them to the best preschools, buying them the latest toys, or acquiescing to the current outrageous fads of slutty or gangsta garb. Raising children, moral molecule by moral molecule, is very time-consuming, hard work. It requires consistent teaching and discipline, as well as demonstrating goodness by our own actions and interactions.

But it's the only way parents can honor their sacred trust to develop children who are lovingly bonded, moral and good.

Dr. Laura Schlessinger, "Which Are Better . . . Smart Kids or Good Kids?" *USA Weekend* magazine (15–17 January 1999), 5.

Teenagers are developing their personal values and beliefs. This is an important step in their lives, but it can cause conflict at home. Relax, take a deep breath, and help them experience this exhilarating trapeze swing.

THINK IT THROUGH

1. When you were in junior high, what values and beliefs that your parents held did you doubt or question? How about in high school? After high school?
2. At what age did you realize that you could think?
3. What was the major cause of your arguments with your parents? What issues did you discuss?
4. Which of your parents' values do you see in yourself? How are your beliefs similar to theirs? Where do they differ? When did you realize that in many ways you had become your parents?
5. What evidence do you see that your teenagers are developing their own values and beliefs?
6. What can you do to help your teenagers build their own faith and not simply parrot what you and your church say?
7. Besides you and your spouse, who else exerts a strong influence on your teenagers?
8. What can you do to be a better listener?
9. What can you do to better model the values you want your kids to have?
10. What improvements would you like to see in your church's youth ministry? What can you do to strengthen that ministry?

Part II

Principles of Effective Parenting

Rules without Relationships Lead to Rebellion

"That's against the rules!"

"I'm sorry, we have rules against that."

"Everyone must follow the rules."

We're surrounded by rules, and we become increasingly aware of those rules as we get older. Our first experiences come at home, where Mommy and Daddy explain how we should eat, when and where we can play, and how we should treat others. Next, schools and teachers present a flood of rules and regulations. We learn how to act in class, what actions will land us in trouble, and what is expected of us. Added soon to this list, of course, are the rules for sports and music and borrowing library books.

As teenagers, we become painfully aware of actions that can bring detentions or suspension from school and of activities that can usher us quickly into the legal system. And then there are all those "rules of the road" hammered into us during Driver's Ed.

Entering the adult world, we soon learn that those previously learned rules and regulations are just the tip of the iceberg as we embark on a chosen career, get married, start a family, buy a home, and save for retirement. Every major decision and every contract comes with a fresh set of rules.

The list of regulations is unending. In fact, a quick search of the Internet can yield more than 1.2 million Web sites dealing with rules of one type or another: rules for golf, baseball, and tiddlywinks; "Audience Etiquette: Golden Rules"; "Mississippi Court Rules"; "Yorkshire Association of Change Ringers— Rules and Regulations"; and, of course, thousands of rules from the IRS, OSHA, Civil Service, and other government agencies, to name just a few.

Certainly, rules rule.

Because teenagers push against limits and react against rules (remember, they're seeking autonomy and moving toward adulthood—it's their job), some parents can become psyched out. In an attempt to avoid conflict and to be their kids' "buddies," these parents back off and try the laissez-faire approach, eliminating most if not all rules. But rules are important—all of us, especially teenagers, need limits.

At the opposite pole, some parents eagerly embrace this truth and create a long list of house rules. Their motto seems to be "The more rules, the better." But this approach usually alienates teenagers who are learning to think for themselves and want to make their own decisions.

THE IMPORTANCE OF RULES

Believe it or not, even though they don't act like it, teenagers actually *want* rules. It's a well-kept secret, something that kids will never tell you directly and one they will deny if you ever confront them with it, but it's true. They need rules and limits. Without parameters, teenagers will have no sense of security and will not know what is expected of them. Without clear rules, they will eventually act out in inappropriate ways, exhibit behavior problems, and, perhaps, even get into trouble with the law.

Young people also want established rules because they don't want parents to tell them what to do all the time. Little children don't mind having constant verbal direction and guidance

A Biblical Principle

The critical relationship between rules and relationships can be compared to the relationship between law and grace in Scripture. Under the old covenant, God's people were required to live in strict adherence to the law, and the result was rebellion. But under the new covenant, God's people have been invited into a new kind of relationship with the Father through Jesus Christ, who paid the penalty for our sins on the cross. As the old hymn puts it, "What a friend we have in Jesus!" And because of this new relationship with Christ, we gladly follow him in obedience. The *relationship* makes it possible to obey the *rules!*

—Wayne Rice

from Mommy or Daddy, but teenagers *do* mind. So rules act as a kind of third party in the authority structure (like the Constitution), especially when teenagers have had some say in creating those rules.

Generally speaking, young children respond to parental power and authority without questioning it. In contrast, teenagers want to know Why? or Why not? Rather than a dictatorship, teens want the home to be a democracy. They will even settle for a benevolent dictatorship in which the parents inform them of the rules ahead of time and explain why the rules are important and necessary. If the rules are reasonable (which they should be), most teens will have no problem with them. Even though adolescents may occasionally ignore regulations, guidelines, and laws or willfully break them, they still want and need rules.

CREATING RULES

Some rules need to be created solely by parents, but many can be negotiated and decided on with teenagers' input. Each family will have a different set of rules. For example:

- You have to be home on weekend nights by eleven.
- You may not have friends in the house after school when we are not here unless it's Julie Longwell.
- All of your dirty laundry should be put in the laundry hamper.

Every rule should also have a corresponding, agreed-upon consequence if it is broken. The most important principle here is that parents and teens know ahead of time what is acceptable and what is not, and what happens when specific rules are not obeyed.

Our rules should be clear and specific. For example, with a rule about being on time for dinner, everyone should understand what "on time" means. We need to be specific. Most rules are broken because the rule maker and the rule breaker have different ideas about what the rule means.

Likewise, in two-parent families, Mom and Dad should present a united front. Teenagers can be formidable opponents in arguments. They have a knack for finding a crack in parents' logic or using one parent against the other. But parents who agree regarding rules and requests are less likely to be divided and conquered and ultimately lose the battle. Whenever possible, Mom and Dad should confer and agree ahead of time on the rules and their consequences before talking with their teenagers or getting into disputes. If an argument arises, they should call a time-out and have a parental conference before proceeding.

Only Two Rules Needed

Your family may only need these two rules:
1. Family members will always treat each other with respect.
2. Family members will take full responsibility for their own actions.

Or . . . you may need two rules with a little more detail:

1. Family members *will not:*
- Engage in any kind of physical violence in the home
- Use abusive language (cursing, insults, put-downs, slams,

- Leave home without permission or without informing one of the parents
- Skip classes at school
- Use drugs of any kind (including alcohol)
- Be dishonest (which includes lying, leaving out important information, and so on)
- Be involved in any immoral behavior (sex outside of marriage, use of pornography, and so on)
- Become associated or identified with people who are involved in crime, drug use, or any other unacceptable behavior

2. Family members *will*:
   - Respect and obey those in authority (parents, teachers, other adults)
   - Complete chores and other household responsibilities as required
   - Attend all regularly scheduled family events (such as meals, church on Sunday, birthday and holiday celebrations, and so on)
   - Finish homework assignments before watching TV or engaging in other leisure activities
   - Clean up after themselves when leaving an area shared by other family members
   - Respect curfews
   - Volunteer to contribute to the family (doing things not asked of them) on a regular basis

Many parents make the mistake of believing that some rules are so obvious that they can "go without saying." These are the same parents who can't understand how their child ended up pregnant or addicted to drugs. We shouldn't assume that our kids can read our minds or will automatically know what to do or not do. Instead, we should be explicit and forthright about values and behaviors that are important to us and the family. One researcher found that many teenagers who were engaging in premarital sex did so simply because "no one ever told them not to."

If necessary, we can write out the rules and hang them on the wall. Some parents sign the rules and have the kids sign them as well—as a covenant or contract between them. Such a document can be revised and amended as needed, but its existence serves as a reference point for problems that may arise in the future, and parents won't be left to argue, shout, or unilaterally impose rules or punishment. Just as businesses have employee manuals and mission statements to ensure that everyone is working toward a common goal, so a family may need to write down important guidelines to keep the family functioning properly. A written set of rules or a "family constitution" can prevent misunderstandings.

Private Rental Room Agreement

Private Room in a lovely neighborhood. Located near major entertainment centers and shopping areas. Large backyard with swimming pool, spa, trampoline, barbecue, and many other outdoor amenities.

The benefits of living in this beautiful area are many. The private room includes one of two floor plans that come with either two single beds or one double bed plus drawer and closet space needed to live and dress comfortably. Storage space in the attic will be provided for small boxes, and space in the three-car garage will be allotted for larger items. A two-sink bathroom adjacent to the rooms will be provided for your convenience. There is a full-sized pool table in the living area along with many other conveniences, such as guitars, oak piano, TV with VCR, stereo system including a six-CD player, computer with Internet access, Nintendo 64, tools of all shapes and sizes, microwave, refrigerators, freezer, all kitchen appliances and utensils, washer and dryer, and much more.

The in-house attendants will provide many items for your benefit such as: toothpaste, soap, toilet paper, shampoo, laundry soap, hair spray, makeup (if needed), bottled water, mega amounts of nutritious food cooked to order or ready for your consumption from the food storage units located strategically in the kitchen area, milk, juice, sodas, spices, and many other miscellaneous items that are required in a household.

The in-house attendants will also be responsible for payments of the following utilities: natural gas for water heating, heating the house, air conditioning, cooking, and so on; electricity for running fans, televisions, computers, lights, and such; water for showers, drink\ing, toilet flushing, washing dishes, bathing, swimming, washing clothes, and so forth.

The $250 weekly rental charge for the above accommodations will be waived in exchange for the renter's agreement to perform the following duties:

- Maintaining your living area to the satisfaction of the attendants
- Keeping the bathroom clean to the satisfaction of the attendants
- Making sure the kitchen is free of your mess to the satisfaction of the attendants

- Attending school regularly and responsibly completing all homework assignments
- Completing chores assigned to you to the satisfaction of the attendants
- Complying completely with other house rules, such as curfews and meal schedules

The in-house attendants will be at your service for many things, including nursing you when you are sick, washing your clothes if you put them in the dirty clothes hamper, but they will not tolerate any disrespectful or argumentative attitudes, shouting, or verbal abuse (curses, insults, or threats).

Noncompliance with any of these requirements will result in a $10 fine, payable immediately or deducted from your allowance.

Repeated or consistent noncompliance will result in a termination of this agreement, and you will either, (1) begin paying rent or (2) be given two weeks in which to find another place to live.

If the requirements listed above are acceptable to the renter, please sign the space below:

X _____

Date: _____

By Tim and Teresa Loza. Thanks to Doug Fields for passing it on to us.

MAKING RULES WORK

Rules are important, but we should remember this: Rules will not act as the glue that holds a family together. That's the mistake made by parents who love rules and think the more rules they have, the better their chances will be of creating well-behaved children and peace and harmony in the home. Just because we have rules doesn't mean that our teenagers will obey those rules. In fact, the opposite will often occur. Some teenagers see rules as challenges; they are meant to be broken.

To make rules work, we need two things: consequences and relationships. As we'll deal with consequences in chapter 11, we'll focus on relationships now. Remember the principle behind this chapter: *Rules without relationships lead to rebellion.* Or, put positively, the better the relationship we have with our teenagers, the more likely they will be to respect our rules.

RELATIONSHIPS

Just as teenagers need a new kind of rules that will work in their changing view of the world, they also need a new kind of relationship with their parents. Mom and Dad can't function as omnipotent authority figures anymore. Young children respond to power and authority because parents are bigger and stronger, but teenagers respond to relationships.

"But None of My Friends Have to Be Home at Midnight!"

Ever heard that one before? Don't believe it. More often than not, your teenagers' friends don't have the freedom and relaxed rules that they brag about. If you have doubts, a phone call to their parents will usually confirm family standards similar to your own.

But assuming your teenager is telling the truth, your best response will be something like this: "I don't care what goes on in someone else's house. I only care about what goes on in this house." You should never feel pressured to conform to other people's rules and values if you believe in your heart that your rules are important, reasonable, and appropriate.

Adolescents will abide by set rules if they have a good relationship with the rule makers. For example, if teens like a teacher (and the teacher likes them), there's a good chance they will work hard and do the best they can in that class. But if they don't like a teacher, they will more than likely find it difficult to be motivated to perform up to their capabilities.

How Well Do You Know Your Teenager?

1. Who is your teen's best friend?
2. What is your teen's favorite radio station?
3. Does your teen have a nickname at school? What is it?
4. Who is your teen's greatest hero?
5. What is your teen's most prized possession?
6. What is your teen's biggest worry?
7. What career is your teen considering?
8. What class at school does your teen like the most?
9. With what adult outside the home does your teen have a good relationship?
10. What does your teen like to do in his or her spare time?

If you answered 9 or 10 correctly, way to go! You are a top-notch observer.

If you answered 7 or 8, you're doing well . . . but there's room for improvement.

If you answered 6 or less, uh-oh. You need to sit down and have a chat with your teenager and get acquainted.

Think, for a moment, of your favorite teachers or coaches during junior high and senior high. Why did you like them?

Most will answer that these men and women were firm, yet friendly; they had high expectations, but they were fair; they insisted on a strong, best effort, but they genuinely cared for their students. Whether it was choir or cross-country, Spanish or soccer, we worked hard and excelled for teachers and coaches who expected discipline, pushed us to do our best, and really liked us at the same time.

This means that anything we do to improve the relationships we have with our teenagers will increase the likelihood that they will respect the rules we believe are important.

Youth workers know this is true. If a teenage boy in a youth group is causing trouble and breaking the rules, the best strategy is not to shout him down, insult him, punish him, or ban him from future meetings. Instead, the best way to solve the discipline problem is to get to know that young man and build a relationship with him. Once the boy is on the team, he will be less likely to be a discipline problem because he will have a relationship to protect. The youth leader will have become his friend, and friends don't mess up their friends' meetings.

It has been said that there are two ways to open an egg. One way is to hit it with a hammer, and the other is to keep it warm—which will likely result in the egg opening itself. Similarly, there are two ways to get our teenagers to abide by our rules. We can hit them with a hammer (yell, shout, punish), or we can keep them warm with a relationship—which will likely result in kids who are more responsive to our parental authority.

MAKING RELATIONSHIPS WORK

Parents *can* have good relationships with their teenagers, even as the teens are pulling away and seeking autonomy. Most teenagers want to have a better (but different) relationship with their parents. To build good relationships and make these relationships work, we should take the following steps.

Talk, Don't Communicate

In my opinion, the term "communication" has been much overused in the literature on parenting. We are told we need to communicate with our offspring, and we are often given various formulas for saying things in the "right" way. . . . Rather than learn to follow a script when conversing with our teenagers, we need simply to talk. The term "communication" suggests that we have a specific message and our only problem is having the time, the opportunity, or the right words to get that message across. But I have found the problem is somewhat different. The true problem is that teenagers are really not quite sure what it is that is bothering them. They need to talk in a rather free-wheeling way in order to discover what they want to say to us.

We need to allow time for talk with our teenagers without pressuring them to "say what they have to say" and to get on with it. Such talk, which can initially center on music, films, sports, friends, or politics, can help young people find out what they are really thinking and feeling.

David Elkind, *All Grown Up and No Place to Go* (Reading, MA: Addison-Wesley, 1984), 204.

First, *we should change the nature of the dialogue we have with our kids.* Too much of the dialogue between parents and teenagers is negatively toned, one-way communication—parents issuing commands and warnings, platitudes, and lectures. If we continue to talk down to our kids, they will more than likely rebel. If we relate to them as young adults, however, and speak to them with more respect, they will be more likely to act and respond in an adult manner.

Think of your conversations with other adults. How do you talk to your friends? You probably would not use these familiar phrases: "How many times do I have to tell you . . . !"; "You should know better than that!"; "Look at me when I'm talking to you!"; "I'm not asking you, I'm telling you!"; "Do you have to go out looking like a slob?"

When you talk with your friends, what do you talk about? Most likely, you discuss your day, what's happening at work, what you just read in the newspaper, or the latest sports or entertainment news, or you might share a new joke or bit of gossip. That's the way adults talk. We should let our teens participate in that kind of dialogue. It will help to equip our kids with good interpersonal skills, and we will begin to build a relationship that is less adult-to-child and more adult-to-adult. Such relationships can develop into true friendships. We should talk *across*, not *down*, to our teens.

Second, *we should learn to listen to our teenagers.* An important part of healthy dialogue, of course, is listening—the key to good communication. Most parents have difficulty listening to their teenage children. And most teenagers list as their top complaint against parents: "They never listen to me!"

Parents have to learn how to listen to their teenagers. When our kids were very young, they probably rambled on and on almost endlessly about trivial matters that are not very interesting to adults. When the small child runs into the room shouting, "Mommy, Mommy, guess what happened!" we get all excited, only to learn that the big event was a Bugs Bunny cartoon on TV that the child wants to describe in great detail for the next thirty minutes. It can be difficult to listen to little children and their concerns for very long.

The Listening FAD

F   Focus. Give your teen your undivided attention. Stop what you're doing and pay attention.

A   Accept. Let your teen know that you are glad he or she is communicating with you. Smile, lean forward, show your interest.

D   Draw out. Ask questions. Get more information. This lets your teen know that you really care!

Teenagers, however, need someone to listen. Unfortunately, many parents have grown used to paying little attention to what their children have to say.

Listening takes patience, especially when we know where a comment or a question is headed. Instead of thinking of our response while the teenager is talking or, worse, interrupting with a quick answer, we need to focus on the individual and take seriously what he or she is saying.

Listening has rightly been called "the language of love." It's how one person shows another that he or she is loved and appreciated, taken seriously, and respected. If a husband wants to express love to his wife, the best way is not with hugs and kisses or gifts, but with a listening ear. Every person wants to be treated with respect, to be understood, to know that his or her feelings and desires count for something. Teenagers are no different. They have a great desire to be treated with respect.

In a speech to youth workers a few years ago, sociologist H. Stephen Glenn made this insightful comment: "If you will take teenagers seriously and treat them with great dignity and respect, they in turn will give you great power and authority over them." This speaks directly to the point. If we want teenagers to respect our rules, we need to treat them with respect. When we do this, they will give us the authority we desire.

Breakfast with Dad

I read somewhere that the average father spends about three minutes a day interacting with his kids. I didn't think it applied to me (I'm not an average father, am I?). But as my kids started getting older and busier, and as I started getting older and busier, I realized that I wasn't even getting my three minutes on some days.

So, when our oldest son, Nathan, entered junior high school, I asked him if he would be interested in going out for breakfast with me once a week. "We'll go out to a restaurant, and then I'll take you to school," I offered. He liked the idea, mostly because he liked the idea of going out for breakfast. Being with me was not the attraction.

We decided on Wednesday mornings at six-thirty—he had to be at school by seven-thirty. I promised myself that I wouldn't use that time to lecture him, nag him, scold him, or give him a new list of chores to do. I wanted to use that time to listen and to find out what was going on in his life. I also thought he might be interested in what was going on in my life.

We went out for breakfast every Wednesday during his seventh-grade year. And we decided to do it again when he entered eighth grade. This continued all the way through high school. When he got his driver's license (and a car to drive), we took two cars. For six years straight, we did breakfast together almost every week. When my son Corey reached junior high, we did the same thing—on Thursday mornings.

Why? Because I felt we needed some one-on-one time on a regular basis. Our lives got so busy that we were like ships in the night, missing each other entirely during the week. So we made sure that we were at least getting a little time each week to sit down and talk.

We didn't have incredibly deep conversations every week. In fact, some weeks we didn't talk much at all. Maybe one of us was in a lousy mood, or we were both tired, or we just didn't have much to say. But every so often, we connected—some positive dialogue took place, some significant life sharing went on, and it made all those other nonproductive times worth it.

Breakfast once a week isn't a cure-all to the problem of poor parent-teen relationships, but for Nate and Corey and me, it was a step in the right direction that helped keep us closer during their teen years.

—Wayne Rice

Third, *we should take time to be with our kids.* Kids spell love T-I-M-E.

These days, much has been made of the importance of *"quality* time." Simply stated, this means that parents should try to make every moment count with their children. Certainly there is some truth in this, and it is an important emphasis. Just being in the same house or even in the same room with a child doesn't mean that a parent is spending time *with* that child. Unfortunately, many parents are so preoccupied with paying bills, watching TV, reading the paper, or working on a project that they hardly notice their kids. These parents might insist that they spend time with their children, but it's merely *quantity*, with no quality.

Instead of just "putting in our time" at home, we should focus on each individual and take advantage of teachable moments; we should try to make our time at home significant and meaningful.

But the quality vs. quantity time is a false dichotomy because it's virtually impossible to have quality time *without* quantity time. Consider the businessman who returns from a trip, breezes into the house, corners his teenage son, and insists on having an in-depth discussion. Or how much success do you think a mother would have in suddenly asking her eighth-grade daughter about her views on sex? Timing is everything. We can't predict every social crisis, question about faith, neighborhood tragedy, or reaction to world news. When those events happen, we need to be ready to sit, listen, counsel, and, at times, teach. (The Littleton, Colorado, tragedy at Columbine High School is an example of an event that merits in-depth sharing between parents and teens.) But we can't do that if we're not there. Quality moments occur in the context of hours together.

We can also spend concentrated amounts of time with each teen, going out to breakfast or lunch together on a weekly basis, taking kids along occasionally on business trips, spending a day or weekend shopping, fishing, or doing another activity together. Those hours and days can be filled with quality.

How do you spend time with your kids? Sometimes we have to be creative. One dad arranged a train trip with his son, just

Forty Relationship-Building Ideas

Go to a ball game together.

Have devotions together.

Go bowling.

Work together on a service project.

Go to a movie together.

Go on a hike or cross-country skiing.

Ride bikes.

Go to the mall.

Have breakfast at a restaurant.

Build a model airplane.

Learn something new on the computer.

Shop 'til you drop.

Visit a college.

Read through a book of the Bible together.

Cook a meal together.

Go fishing.

Do lunch.

Fly a kite. Better yet, build a kite, then fly it.

Attend a concert.

Play video games.

Play laser tag.

Bake and decorate a birthday cake for someone.

Play a round of golf.

Go to an amusement park.

Go camping.

Chop wood.

Go hunting with a camera.

Exercise together.

Play board games until two in the morning.

Make a quilt.

Go rock climbing.

Visit a museum.

Look at old pictures.

Collect stamps.

Go swimming.

Make a video.

Make a snowman or go sledding.

Go for a walk on the beach or in the park.

Do homework together.

Visit someone in the hospital.

the two of them, visiting five cities with major league ball-parks, going to baseball games, staying in hotels, eating out, and having fun together. According to the sixteen-year-old, "It changed everything between my dad and me. We have a great relationship."

FRIENDS FOR LIFE

Here's a little extra incentive for working on our relationships with our teenagers: The relationships we establish with our teenagers today will serve as the foundation for the relationships we will have with them for the rest of our lives.

Do you want to be friends with your adult children—to have good relationships with them when they are on their own? It's a sad truth that millions of adult children continue to have strained relationships with their parents, simply because that's all they experienced during their teen years. There's no better time than now to begin developing that new kind of bond that will continue into adulthood.

THINK IT THROUGH

1. What rules did your parents set during your teenage years that, looking back, you are glad they did?
2. Which rules do you think were unnecessary? Why?
3. Why do teenagers need rules?
4. What are the most important rules in your home? Why are they important? How did you decide on them?
5. How have your rules changed as your children have gotten older?
6. What kind of relationship did you have with your parents during junior high school? During senior high school?

7. How has your relationship with your parents changed over the years?
8. How do your kids know that you love them?
9. How much time do you spend at home (awake) during a typical week? How much of that time do you spend interacting with your kids?
10. What can you do to spend more time with each child at home?
11. What can you do to spend time with each child outside the house?
12. What's the most recent *quality* moment you had with a teenage son or daughter?

Chapter 8

Catch Your Teenager in the Act of Doing Something Good

Marge and Ted shut the car doors and slowly walk to the church. They know they need this seminar on parents and teens more than most, but they are having some second thoughts about attending. Julie, their junior higher, has been giving them fits at home. She has been uncooperative and argumentative, refusing to do anything they ask unless they force her to, including homework. This change seems to have happened suddenly, almost on the day she turned thirteen several months ago. Before then, Julie had been a sweet child and a good student, almost the opposite of her present attitude and demeanor. The relationship between them and Julie has progressively deteriorated, and now she is driving them crazy. *How* *much of these struggles should we reveal?* they think. *Will anyone understand?*

Just before they reach the door, a voice rings out behind them. "Marge. Ted." It's Alice Langston, hurrying up the sidewalk. Although they haven't known Alice very long, Ted and Marge have developed a close friendship with her, a single mom with two toddlers. Alice works part-time at the church and is helping with the seminar logistics. As she catches up to them, she continues, "I'm so glad you're here. I know you'll have much to share with the others. I am so impressed with your Julie—she is such a doll. And so polite and conscientious. I hope you don't mind my using her to baby-sit so often!"

Marge and Ted smile and mumble their thanks as they open the church door and follow Alice in. Is she talking about the same girl—*their* Julie?—they wonder.

Many parents can relate to Marge and Ted's experience. When someone tells them what a great kid they have (for example, "He was such a gentleman" or "She really impressed us with her thoughtfulness"), these parents think the person must have their child confused with somebody else.

They don't. For reasons that are hard to understand, it's frequently easier for other people to notice the good in our teenagers than it is for us. That's why the action stated in the title of this chapter ("Catch Your Teenager in the Act of Doing Something Good") is so difficult for most parents.

Actually, many parents just aren't paying close enough attention to their teens. They have built-in "botch detectors" that go off whenever the teenagers make mistakes, break rules, disobey commands, or do anything else they find offensive (and this happens quite often). At the same time, they seem to be blind to anything good that their teens do. In fact, some parents seem to think that their only role is to point out misbehavior in their children and, then, to correct it immediately.

Just a few years ago, the situation was quite different. Think back to when your son or daughter was a child. Chances are good that most all of his or her accomplishments were rewarded with praise: "What a big boy you are!"; "Look at how well you tied your shoes!"; "Wow! Look how neatly you printed your name." And pictures and tests from school and church were posted on the refrigerator.

Compare that with what teenagers commonly hear from their parents:

- "There are things *growing* in your room!"
- "I hope you have a kid someday just like you!"
- "I'm not asking you, I'm *telling* you!"
- "I can't believe you would be so stupid!"
- "Do you have to go out looking like a slob?"
- "What part of *no* don't you understand?"
- "Because I'm your mother, that's why!"
- "Look at me when I'm talking to you!"
- "Do I look like a bank?"

Remember how good you felt when your boss, your spouse, or a good friend told you how much they appreciated something you did? Affirmation is a wonderful gift that we parents can give to our teenagers. We should remember this principle and put it into practice: We should catch our kids in the act of doing something good.

TEENS NEED AFFIRMATION

Teenagers are no different from anyone else. They need encouragement, especially from their parents. Mark Twain is purported to have said, "I can live for two months on one good compliment." While that speaks to the power of a good compliment, teenagers need more than one per month. They not only need affirmation from their parents, but they also want it.

The next time you watch a college football game on TV, notice how almost every player who makes a great play goes to the bench, takes off his helmet, looks straight into the camera, and says, "Hi, Mom!" So it is with teenagers. You can bet that whenever they do something good, they are hoping their folks are watching. More than anyone else, teens want to please their parents—and to know that their parents are proud of them.

Affirmation Builds Relationships

In chapter 7, we discussed the importance of staying close to your kids, keeping the relationship warm. Affirmation is one of the best ways to do that.

Everyone enjoys being around people who like them. It's natural to be attracted to positive, affirming people who enjoy our

---

My Dad Laughed at My Jokes

One of the fondest memories I have of my father is that he always laughed at my jokes. I never realized how difficult that is to do until my own teenage children started telling jokes. They aren't very funny most of the time. My jokes weren't very funny either, but I'll never forget Dad's laughter. His laughter encouraged me to keep on telling jokes, which I did. This became a very useful skill when I became a youth pastor and public speaker. I will always be grateful to my father for the gift of his laughter.

—Wayne Rice

company. On the other hand, we probably won't spend much time with people who are negative and critical. No one wants to hang out with someone who is constantly criticizing, pointing out faults, and making them feel bad about themselves. Teens are no different. Kids who are constantly being criticized by their parents have a natural tendency to distance themselves. It's a matter of self-preservation. If your kids bolt when they see you coming, it may be because you're not fun to be around—they aren't getting the affirmation they need.

Affirmation Encourages Positive Behavior

Most parents want their teenagers to be more polite, more mature, more thoughtful, more helpful, and more responsible. Many try to instill these qualities in their children by nagging, correcting, punishing, and lecturing—usually with little discernible success. Actually, the best way to encourage positive behavior is to give positive feedback whenever the positive behavior occurs.

Believe it or not, at times our teenagers make the effort to do what is right. No matter how feeble the attempt, we will miss an opportunity for growth if we don't applaud the effort. Unfortunately, many parents fail to take advantage of such opportunities because they are closet perfectionists. They expect their children to perform up to their extremely high expectations. Teenagers rarely do things perfectly, however. They may try to be helpful yet bungle the job. They may make an attempt to be thoughtful yet say something really stupid. They may try hard to get good grades yet only produce B's and C's. If we only focus on the mistakes, our teenagers will more than likely stop trying. But if we congratulate them on their efforts, they will try again in the future, perhaps with greater success.

Before Parents Know It,
the Need to Nag Is Over

A young mother writes: "I know you've written before about the empty-nest syndrome—that lonely period after the children are grown and gone. Right now, I'm up to my eyeballs in laundry and muddy boots. The baby is teething; the boys are fighting. My husband just called and said to eat without him, and I fell off my diet. Lay it on me again, will you?"

OK. One of these days, you'll shout, "Why don't you kids grow up and act your age!" And they will. Or, "You guys get outside and find yourselves something to do . . . and don't slam the door!" And they won't.

You'll straighten up the boys' bedroom neat and tidy—bumper stickers discarded, bedspread tucked and smooth, toys displayed on the shelves, hangers in the closet, animals caged. And you'll say out loud, "Now I want it to stay this way." And it will.

You'll prepare a perfect dinner with a salad that hasn't been picked to death and a cake with no finger traces in the icing, and you'll say, "Now, there's a meal for company." And you'll eat it alone.

You'll say: "I want complete privacy on the phone. No dancing around. No demolition crews. Silence! Do you hear?" And you'll have it.

No more plastic tablecloths stained with spaghetti. No more bedspreads to protect the sofa from damp bottoms. No more gates to stumble over at the top of the basement steps. No more clothespins under the sofa. No more playpens to arrange a room around. No more anxious nights under a vaporizer tent. No more sand on the sheets or Popeye movies in the bathrooms. No more iron-on patches, wet shoe-strings, tight boots, or rubber bands for ponytails.

Imagine. A lipstick with a point on it. No baby-sitter for New Year's Eve. Washing only once a week. Seeing a steak that isn't ground. Having your teeth cleaned without a baby on your lap.

No PTA meetings. No car pools. No blaring radios. No one washing her hair at 11 o'clock at night. Having your own roll of Scotch tape.

Think about it. No more Christmas presents out of toothpicks and library paste. No more sloppy oatmeal kisses. No more tooth fairy. No giggles in the dark. No knees to heal, no responsibility.

Only a voice crying, "Why don't you grow up?" and the silence echoing, "I did."

Erma Bombeck, Universal Press Syndicate, 1996.

Affirmation Builds Self-Esteem

As we have mentioned several times, low self-esteem is a common malady among today's teenagers. The causes for this lack of self-esteem are many: the perception of being "totally unnecessary," the dramatic physical and mental changes occurring, the search for identity, rejection by friends and other peers, a lack of adult "tools," doubts about their faith, arguments over the home rules, and other factors. Millions of kids with unlimited potential have come to believe that they simply don't have what it takes to become successful in life. Somehow they have become convinced that they are incapable of accomplishing anything worthwhile or significant. When kids start feeling this way, they often lose interest in school, extracurricular activities, church, and other positive skill-building groups and events.

Lacking motivation to participate or succeed in anything worthwhile, they just hang out with friends or get into trouble.

Low self-esteem can become a vicious cycle of despair for teenagers. When kids start thinking of themselves as losers, they generally communicate this view of themselves to everyone else around them, making the problem worse. Rather than encouraging these young people, parents, teachers, and friends begin relating to them as losers, as "problem" teenagers.

Teens who feel discouraged and succumb to feelings of low self-esteem tend to seek recognition and significance (even notoriety) in areas where they are more certain of being accepted. They may get involved in negative behaviors such as fighting, drinking, using drugs, vandalizing, using rude language, disrupting class, or being sexually promiscuous. Research has confirmed that teenagers who have a low self-concept are the true "at risk" kids. These kids are most vulnerable to negative peer pressure and self-destructive behaviors.

Ironically, some of the most unmotivated, at-risk teenagers are those from homes with very successful and highly motivated parents. These parents may spend a considerable amount of time trying to get their kids to become high achievers, but with little success. Their intentions may be good, but their methods often provoke resistance or foster even greater discouragement. Badgering, threatening, or begging teenagers to make something of themselves is rarely effective. Instead, this approach inevitably results in power struggles, conflict, and rebellion.

Unfortunately, modern society puts a great deal of emphasis on individuals' mistakes. We hear mostly bad news about celebrities, sports stars, politicians, and even preachers. Most humor in television situation comedies and by stand-up comedians is based on the put-down. One researcher found that the average teenager gets "dissed" (insulted, criticized, or "slammed") ten times for every one time he or she is praised. This, of course, is one of the ways teenagers try to make themselves feel superior— they cut other people down.

Some parents fall into the same trap and focus primarily on teenagers' weaknesses and liabilities. Actually, this may be an attempt by those parents to establish their own superiority. Have you ever found it hard to admit that your teenager might be doing better than you in some area?

Home should be the one place in the world where kids feel safe from "dissing." Loving parents should do everything they can to provide their children with a safe place, a "home on the range" where "seldom is heard a discouraging word." Healthy homes are safe places where kids hear more positive feedback than negative. All kids need and want that.

WHAT TO DO

Here are a few tips on affirmation:

Be there when they do something good. This involves the "quantity" time discussed earlier and means taking an interest in the things that our kids are interested in. We should go to their activities, games, and performances, giving them the unmistakable support of our presence. This can be tough for today's busy parents, but teenagers rarely have the perspective to understand why a business meeting is more important than they are. A teen's world is a lot smaller than an adult's. When parents can't be part of it, they get the message loud and clear: I am not important to Mom and Dad.

Practice and use the vocabulary of love. Some parents say, "I don't really know how to communicate to my teenager that I love him." Well, there is hardly a better way than to use the English language. A wide variety of words and phrases express love to a young person, including the phrase "I love you." Many parents, especially fathers, however, have a hard time expressing their feelings in clear, unequivocal statements. We should get in the habit of using phrases like those found in "The Vocabulary of Love" sidebar in this chapter. We can practice

Got a Minute?

A mother who had just finished reading a book on parenting was convicted about some of the things she had been failing to do as a parent. Feeling this conviction, she went upstairs to talk to her son. When she got upstairs, all she could hear coming from his room was the loud sound of his drums. She had a message she wanted to deliver, but when she knocked on the door, she got cold feet.

"Got a minute?" she said, as her son answered her knock.

"Mom, you know I always have a minute for you," said the boy.

"You know, Son, I . . . I . . . I just love the way you play the drums."

He said, "You do? Well, thanks, Mom!"

She got up and started back downstairs. Halfway down, she realized that she had not conveyed the message she had intended, so back she went to his door and once again knocked. "It's Mom again! Do you have another minute?" she said.

He said, "Mom, like I told you before, I always have a minute for you."

She went over and sat on the bed. "When I was here before I had something I wanted to tell you and I didn't get it said. What I really meant to say was . . . your dad and I . . . we just really think you're great."

He said, "You and Dad?"

She said, "Yes, your dad and I."

"Okay, Mom. Thanks a lot."

She left and was once again halfway down the stairs when she realized she had gotten closer to the message she intended, but had still not told her boy that she loved him. So up the stairs again she went, back to the door and this time he heard her coming. Before she could ask, he shouted, "Yeah, I have a minute!"

Mom sat down on the bed once more. "You know, Son, I've tried this twice now and I haven't gotten it out. What I really came up here to tell you is this. I love you. I love you with all my heart. Not Dad and I love you, but I love you."

He said, "Mom, that's great. I love you too." He gave her a hug.

She started out of the room and was back at the head of the stairs when her son stuck his head out of his room and said, "Mom . . . got a minute?"

She laughed and said, "Sure."

"Mom," he said, "did you just come from a seminar?"

David Jeremiah, quoted in Alice Gray, *Stories from the Heart* (Gresham, OR: Vision House, 1996), 175–76.

these phrases over and over again, in the mirror if necessary, and then use them frequently on our teenagers. No communication is more direct and clear than words spoken from the heart.

Treat teenagers courteously. Parents should say "please" and "thank you" instead of just giving orders. And we should ask permission before using what belongs to our kids (this teaches, by example, the importance of respecting others' belongings).

We should respect our teenagers' privacy and avoid listening in on their telephone conversations or barging into their rooms without knocking. Also, we should not commit them to anything (like baby-sitting) without consulting with them first. We would act this way with any person outside the family. Why not treat our own kids with the same courtesy? If we do, we'll find that they will develop much more self-respect.

The Vocabulary of Love

- "Clean your room!"
- "Grow up!"
- "Why can't you be like your sister!"
- "Where did you get a stupid idea like that?"

These are only a few ways we destroy a teenager's self-esteem. Instead, substitute phrases like those below—words that encourage and show understanding. Practice them at home on your kids.

- "I love you."
- "How thoughtful."
- "I know you can do it."
- "That's a good point."
- "You're terrific."
- "That's great!"
- "It sounds like you've given that a lot of thought."
- "Now that's an interesting way of looking at it."
- "You are really improving."
- "I know you'll make the right decision."
- "That was a thoughtful thing to do.

- "Since you're not happy with the situation, what do you think you can do to change it?"
- "I'm proud of you."
- "Let's sit down and talk about it."
- "Now that's really creative."
- "You really are growing up."
- "Way to go!"
- "You seem happy about that."
- "You made the right decision."
- "I've noticed that you've been trying harder."
- "You handled that situation well."
- "Good thinking!"
- "I really appreciate you."
- "That's a normal feeling you have."
- "It sounds like you truly care about your friends."
- "Thanks for your help."
- "I'm going to trust you a lot more."
- "Will you pray for me?"
- "I'm sorry. Will you forgive me?"
- "What's your opinion?"
- "It's easy to make a mistake. What did you learn from it?"
- "I understand."
- "I love you."

Assume the best, not the worst. Some parents just naturally assume the worst before all the evidence is in. For example, "Jeremy is late getting home, but I'm sure he has a good reason. I'll try not to overreact," is a better attitude than, "Jeremy is late getting home. He's probably getting into trouble again! When he gets home, I'm putting him on restriction!" If we expect the worst from our teenagers, that's probably what we'll get. Of course, assuming the best doesn't necessarily mean that we should expect the best *all the time* or we'll be disappointed. Instead, we should just remember the old adage about seeing the glass as half full rather than half empty. It's a matter of perspective. We should presume innocence, that our kids are telling the truth, unless the facts prove otherwise. If we give teens the benefit of the doubt first, we'll be much more positive and encouraging people.

Don't expect the teenager to excel at everything. Nothing discourages a teenager faster than a parent whose only standard for success is perfection. Some parents try to live their lives through their children, as if having successful kids will make them look more successful. These parents are more concerned about status and prestige than they are about the welfare of their sons and daughters. They push their teens to meet overly high expectations—starting on the football team, winning the lead role in the school play, having the "right" friends, getting straight A's, or getting into the best college. When teenagers are unable to live up to these unrealistic standards, they naturally conclude that their parents are disappointed in them; this can lead to their just giving up. Overly critical parents may feel uncomfortable encouraging their children in one area because they don't deserve it in another. When the kids fail to measure up in one way, these parents withhold praise for everything. Why encourage, they reason, when there is still so much room for improvement? Such parents may have good intentions, but they discourage their kids from making any effort at all.

Encourage effort and improvement, not just accomplishments. If we wait until our teenagers have accomplished something significant, we may wait a long time. Reaching every worthy goal takes a lot of small steps, and these can be reasons for praise and encouragement along the way. When the teenager improves a grade, makes the team, learns something new on the guitar, or saves some money—applaud these things without expecting more. Many parents will find this a difficult challenge, but it will pay off handsomely.

Remember that mistakes can be affirmed too. This doesn't mean that we should encourage mistakes but that we can appreciate the role of mistakes in the learning process. If we turn every mistake into a catastrophe, we will communicate that mistakes aren't allowed. Instead, we can use mistakes to help our teenagers learn and to reveal our own humanity. Everybody makes mistakes; the proper response is not anger or despair, but discussion, education, and growth. And usually we can compliment the teenager for at least giving it a shot, for trying.

Avoid comparisons. Nothing can be more discouraging to teenagers than to constantly be compared to brothers or sisters (or to anyone else, actually). Every person is unique, with a special personality and set of talents, gifts, and abilities. It's easy for parents to compare children to siblings or friends' children. A mom might say, for example, "Why can't you be like your sister? She had no trouble with geometry." A father might say, "Look, you'll do great at basketball. Give it a try. Your brother sure was great!" In the heat of an argument, a parent might blurt out, "What about Claire? She's the same age as you but she isn't having those kinds of problems." We should resist with all our strength this temptation to compare one child with another. Instead, we should accept each child and help the child develop, mature, and succeed in his or her own way.

Look for character traits and positive behaviors to praise. The goal of affirmation is not to flatter but to encourage. Teenagers will benefit more from "I was really proud of how you handled that situation" than "I like your new hairdo."

Compliments on looks and performance are good, but they can seem quite shallow if we don't go deeper and affirm the *person*. Isn't that what we want from our children? Certainly most parents would agree that it is much more important to rear a child who exhibits honesty, sincerity, compassion, godliness, and other positive character qualities than one who is merely good-looking and who performs well. When we affirm character and good choices, we let our teens know that we appreciate who they are on the inside, and we encourage them to further develop those positive qualities.

Be sincere. This emphasis on affirmation doesn't mean that we should invent compliments, just to express something positive to our teens. We shouldn't say anything that isn't true or that we don't believe. There are plenty of qualities, characteristics, and deeds available for compliments, and we'll see them if we look. Lying or exaggerating will do more harm than good. We should also be careful of speaking in extremes when handing out our affirmations. When a mom tells her daughter, "You're the smartest girl in the whole school," the daughter knows that's not true (even if Mom thinks it is). When a dad tells his son that he played a great game when, in fact, he played poorly, the boy knows that Dad isn't shooting straight with him. It's better to be honest, yet positive. And here's another tip on giving sincere compliments: Express how *you* feel and what *you* appreciated. For example, if a daughter sings a solo in church, Mom or Dad should say something like, "I really enjoyed your solo"; "Your singing means so much to me—thank you"; "I appreciate how you are willing to use your gifts for the Lord"; "I think your voice is getting stronger and better every time I hear you"; or something similar. It would not be good to say something like, "You are the greatest singer!" or "That's the best solo we've ever had around here!" Those last two compliments, though meant well, are so extreme that they are virtually meaningless.

Don't qualify the praise. When giving a compliment, let it stand on its own as a statement of affirmation. We will negate any positive message if we add a "but" to it; for example, "That was great, but . . ." or "Well, it's about time you finally cleaned your room." After a thrilling game in which his daughter was the high scorer and made the winning basket in overtime, one father exclaimed, "Wow! What a game! You were terrific tonight. I noticed, however, that your shot was a little flat." There's a time for affirming and a time for coaching and correcting—we shouldn't mix the two.

Brag on the kids in public. Even though teenagers will sometimes act shy and pretend that they are embarrassed by public praise, down deep they love it when their parents brag on them to friends and extended family. Displaying their artwork, showing newspaper clippings, having pictures of them in action on the desk, even asking them to play their musical instrument for guests, and so forth can be ways to communicate our approval and pride in our children. Of course, we shouldn't overdo it, bragging constantly or pressuring our kids to perform at every occasion (friends and family will soon tire of that as well). But it's good to express parental pride in our teens.

Don't worry about the response. We shouldn't expect our teenagers to respond to our praise with something like, "Thanks, Dad, you're a great father!" or "From now on I will do everything you ask!" Reactions like those would certainly be exceptions. In fact, many teenagers find it hard to even say "thanks" when they receive a compliment. We shouldn't let this discourage us from doing it anyway. When Amber's dad complimented her for being so thoughtful and kind to a friend on the telephone, Amber didn't say, "Thanks, Dad." Instead she said, "Can't anybody have any privacy around here?" But she appreciated the encouragement anyway.

In considering this whole area of affirmation and looking for ways to compliment our teens, it will be helpful to put ourselves in the shoes of a good youth minister. When youth ministers go to high school events to watch kids from the youth group perform or play, they look for what the students do well so they can compliment the kids. When youth director Bob goes to the JV cross-country meet and watches Darin finish dead last, he probably says to Darin, "I really admire you for sticking in there and finishing well. How did you get in condition to run that far?" When youth director Sue goes to a musical and spots Janie in the chorus, she later says to Janie, "I saw that you were in character the whole time. Good job. That's not easy to do." The point is simply this: If we pay attention, we *will* catch our teens in the act of doing something good. And when that happens, we should let them know how much we appreciate who they are and what they have done.

THINK IT THROUGH

1. When you were a teenager, what was the level of your self-esteem?
2. Which adults continued to give you positive affirmation and made you feel good about yourself?
3. What are your favorite phrases in the "vocabulary of love" to *hear*? Which two or three do you use most often?
4. What can you do to treat your teenagers more courteously? Why can this be difficult?
5. In what areas do you expect your teens to excel? How do you communicate your expectations? How successful has this approach been?

6. When did you learn a valuable lesson from making a mistake during your adolescent years?

7. With what other young people are you tempted to compare your teenagers? Why? What can you do to appreciate each of your children's uniqueness?

8. What do you appreciate most about your teenagers' character?

9. For what personal quality or recent action can you sincerely compliment your teens?

10. What have you said or done in the past few months to let others know how proud you are of your kids?

11. How do your children typically respond to your affirmation and praise? How do you feel about those responses?

Pick Your Battles Wisely (Or You'll Be Battling All the Time)

- "This room is a pigsty! I don't know how you can live like this! . . . Look at me when I'm talking. . . . I didn't raise you to be a slob! . . ."
- "The matter's settled as far as I'm concerned. You're not wearing that dress to school, or anywhere for that matter. It makes you look like a slut!"
- "You need more money? What happened to the check you got from Grandma for your birthday? Where do you spend it all anyway? You must think we're made of money, but we're not. It's hard enough trying to keep this family clothed and fed and then have you waste what we give you!"

- "It's twelve-thirty! You know I said to be home at midnight! Why are you late?"
- "Look at these grades! There's no excuse for your getting C's—it's not acceptable. You and I both know that you're smarter than that. You just aren't trying!"
- "I don't like you hanging around with that group. I've heard from other parents about what those kids are like and some of the things they've done. Stay away from them—that's an order!"
- "I thought I told you to pick up your brother after school! . . . You forgot? That's pitiful—how could you forget your brother? Sometimes I don't think you'll ever grow up!"

Parents of teenagers soon discover that *it's possible to stay ticked off twenty-four hours a day.* There's *always* something to be angry about. Even the best young people in the world test their parents' patience, create inconveniences, forget to do as their told, make a mess of things, cost money, take unnecessary risks, behave like barbarians, and, in general, irritate their parents.

OK, that may be a bit exaggerated, but let's admit it—it's easy to stay mad if we choose to do so. And that is precisely the point. How we respond to circumstances is a choice that we make. We can decide whether we will allow our teens' behavior to make life miserable or not. And we can decide whether to react with reason or to overreact with rage.

PERFECTIONIST PARENTS

All parents want to help their teenagers get through their adolescent years without getting into serious trouble. We need not rationalize for worrying about drug abuse, gang violence, vandalism, alcohol, sexual activity, pregnancy, dropping out of school, running away from home, and so on. These serious problems should be given as much attention and energy as we can possibly muster. In any of these serious situations, we certainly should rally the troops and haul out the big guns! The teenager is in danger!

Welcome Home

Picture yourself arriving home in the evening after a hard day. As you turn your car into the driveway, you suddenly have to swerve sharply to avoid running over the new $300 bike you just bought for your teenager. At the edge of the driveway, near where the bike has been abandoned, there are ugly bicycle tire gouges where only just this morning a lovely bed of tulips was growing. As your eyes move to the front porch of the house, you catch sight of several bags of garbage deposited carelessly, the contents spilling out over the steps. At almost the same moment, you notice that a window in the cellar has been shattered by what looks like the impact of an air rifle pellet.

Appalled, you enter the house and immediately trip over a pile of books in the front hall. As you rush into the kitchen, looking for the teenage child who you know is responsible for all this mess and destruction, you see that the dirty dishes from an afternoon snack are still sitting on the kitchen table, alongside a report from the school guidance counselor complaining that homework is not being done. From upstairs comes the ear-splitting blast of rock music.

You race up the stairs to confront your adolescent, and as you fling open the door, the smell of dirty sneakers almost blows you back into the hall. And there, wearing a pair of tattered jeans and a T-shirt with a death's head imprinted across the chest, astride a pile of dirty laundry, scattered sports equipment, soda cans, extension wires, wet towels, candy bar wrappers, and gym clothes is your very own teenager, looking at you with a big innocent grin from ear to ear.

"Hi Dad! How was your day?"

Lawrence Bauman, *The Ten Most Troublesome Teen-Age Problems and How to Solve Them* (Secaucus, NJ: Birch Lane Press, 1997), 23.

Many other teen behaviors, however, while bothersome, are rarely dangerous or fatal—either for the teenager or for the parents. Actually, the only factor that might make these behaviors fatal is us, the parents! When we elevate small problems into big ones, we run the risk of damaging the relationship, alienating our teenagers, and provoking rebellion.

This warning is addressed particularly to idealistic and perfectionist parents who are determined that their children perform and measure up to the highest possible standards. Nothing's wrong with having high standards, of course, but problems arise whenever one person holds another to an unrealistic or even impossible standard. A perfectionist has been defined as "a person who takes great pains with what he does, and then gives them to everyone else." The perfectionist's creed is, "I would rather be right than happy." Perfectionists are people who want everything their way and aren't happy until everything is. Of course, very little ever is, which is why they are generally unhappy people who only make other people unhappy.

If you suffer from strong perfectionist urges from time to time (as most parents do), it's advisable to suppress those urges while you are living with a teenager. Parents who insist that their teenagers keep their bedrooms squeaky-clean or dress neatly or talk respectfully 100 percent of the time are in for some rough water. Rarely are teenagers able to live up to their own standards, let alone anyone else's, and wise parents will allow for that and try to be understanding and empathetic.

SETTING PRIORITIES

Not all teen behaviors deserve the same response from parents. This may sound obvious, but many moms and dads have a difficult time differentiating between what matters and what doesn't. Recently, *Don't Sweat the Small Stuff* hit the best-seller list for books. That title certainly seems to be wise advice. The subtitle of the book, however, is "And It's All Small Stuff," which is not very wise at all because it implies that we shouldn't worry or be concerned about *anything*. Certainly, some "stuff" is worth sweating over, and the smart parent knows the difference between what is and what isn't worth worrying about.

Here's the point: We should save our energy for issues that really matter. If we get mad, scream and yell, and make a big deal out of everything, we won't be heard when we really need to be heard. Can our teenagers tell the difference between a minor infraction and a serious offense by the tone of our voice or the severity of our response? They should be able to. Sadly, some teenagers grow so accustomed to their parents' outbursts that they no longer take the outbursts or their parents seriously. How those parents respond no longer acts as a deterrent. As the late Erma Bombeck wrote, "I had good material. But I used the same two hour speech for filling the glass too full of milk as I used when they stayed out all night without calling home. The speech lost its effectiveness."[1]

On one particular evening in early February, I witnessed a very distressing basketball game. Our eldest son, who was sixteen at the time, played on a team that was young and inexperienced. That night they were matched with a much more physical and accomplished team. The result was a frustrating, one-sided game. Way beyond the impact of the score, however, was the fact that our young players were bombarded with nasty comments and unkind remarks throughout the game. It was a very negative experience.

When the game finally ended, our son grabbed his coat, trousers, and gym bag and told his coach he was riding home with us. He was exhausted from spending the evening in this demoralizing situation. As our family walked outside, the boys and my husband, John, were a few feet ahead of me. The cold air hit my face, and I suddenly realized that Matthew had not put his coat on yet.

"Matthew, put your coat on," I told him.

The eldest child who usually responded in an immediate manner did nothing. His sweaty, slumping shoulders remained uncovered.

"Matthew, it's cold outside. Please put your coat on," I repeated.

When there was still no response, I prepared to give the order a final time with more conviction. As I began to speak, my second son, Aaron, slipped back a few steps to walk with me.

He reached over, touched my arm and said, "Mom, you've got to know when to hold 'em and know when to fold 'em."

Wow! Wisdom out of the mouths of babes (teens, actually). Aaron was 100 percent correct. I was reacting. I wasn't giving a thinking response. If I had been thinking, I would have realized that at that moment, Matthew did not need my advice about dressing for conditions. Instead, he needed the assurance of my unconditional love.

Kendra Smiley, *Empowered by Choice* (Ann Arbor, MI: Servant Publications, 1998), 158–59.

Fifteen-year-old Drew was caught smoking marijuana after school. When the authorities threatened to call his parents, he responded by saying, "Go ahead, I don't care. My parents are always on my case, anyway. It's no big deal." It didn't really matter to Drew that his parents were upset. They were upset all the time, it seemed. Smoking marijuana was just "one more thing." He was in trouble most of the time anyway, and he had learned to deal with it. He also knew that as soon as he had the chance, he would probably do it again.

Contrast Drew with thirteen-year-old Carlos, who was arrested for shoplifting. When the police called his parents, they were devastated. Their response to Carlos's behavior was clear and unambiguous. Never before had they reacted with such anguish and with such concern for their son's welfare. Not only were tears shed, but there would also be serious consequences for his actions. Carlos got the message immediately. He had committed a grave offense, and he knew that he had hurt his parents deeply—more so than at any other time in his life. Never before had he witnessed his parents so disturbed by his behavior. This made him determined to never let it happen again. And he didn't. Today he is fifty-three years old and the coauthor of this book (his real name is Wayne).

How do we determine what is really worth battling over with our teenagers? Unfortunately there are no formulas that will work for everybody, but one approach is to prioritize those things that are morally wrong. Spilling Coke on the new carpet doesn't deserve the same response as telling a lie. Missing curfew by a few minutes is not the same as cheating on an exam at school. If we will save our energy for those issues that have moral significance, we will not only save ourselves (and our teenagers) a lot of grief, but we will also teach our teenagers the difference between right and wrong.

In *Parenting Isn't for Cowards*, Dr. James Dobson suggests a "Loosen and Tighten Principle." When our children become teenagers, he says, we should "loosen [our] grip on the things that don't have any lasting significance and tighten [our] grip on the things that do."[2] As our kids get older, we should pay less attention to behaviors that aren't truly serious, but *more* attention to those that are. The idea is to become not permissive or uncaring but more focused.

Here's a corollary to that principle: We should say yes to the teenager whenever possible in order to give support to the occasional no. Some parents will say no just because they haven't said it in the last twenty-four hours. If that's the case, eventually our kids will stop asking for permission and just do what they want. If, on the other hand, we generally give our teenagers the benefit of the doubt and the support they need to exercise freedom and good judgment, they will be more apt to hear us when we do find it necessary to exercise our authority. That's not a bad trade-off.

WHAT TO DO

It's easy to encourage parents to choose their battles carefully, to fight over only things that matter. But how can parents

make that happen? Here are some suggestions for positive attitudes and actions that can make a difference.

Picking Battles

Which of the following issues do you think are worth "battling"
over with your teenager?

- hairstyle
- language
- music volume
- lying
- earring (males)
- drug or alcohol use
- messy room
- tattoo(s)
- control of the TV set
- food choices
- time use
- household chores
- spending habits
- friends
- a ten-minute curfew
  violation
- an hour curfew violation
- regular church
  attendance
- clothes
- R-rated movies
- car use
- telephone use
- manners
- body piercing
- sibling relationships
- attitudes
- cigarettes
- homework
- pornographic material
- grades
- other: _____

Insulate the Hot Buttons

What things set you off time and time again? Do you get
upset when your teenager uses your stuff without asking? Or
tracks mud into the house? Or brings the car home with an

empty gas tank? Or forgets to flush the toilet after using it? Or fails to turn out the lights in an empty room to save electricity?

Most parents have dozens of hot buttons like these that, when pushed, can ruin their whole day—not to mention the relationships they have with their teenagers. Most hot buttons are minor irritants that aren't worth the energy it takes to get mad. It's all right to continue reminding kids of problem areas (nagging is permitted) or to hold them accountable for their misdeeds (make them clean the toilet or pay the electric bill), but we don't want to let our anger take over. Instead, we should deal with these sensitive areas calmly and with gentleness. One of these days, when the kids are gone, we will actually miss those muddy footprints.

Identifying these hot buttons will help us prepare for them and react reasonably and responsibly.

Get Some Rest

Raising teenagers can be very tiring. Parents who both work are especially susceptible to exhaustion and burnout. They spend all day on the job or at the office only to come home to messes, complaints, arguments, demands, sibling rivalries, missed curfews, loud music, bad grades, jilted lovers, noisy friends, slammed doors, and more—it's enough to drive a *rested* parent crazy, let alone one who is tired and has nothing left to give. Any unexpected crisis or even minor irritant can set off a torrent of emotion.

Here's some advice. When you come home and things are in chaos, don't do anything right away. Get some rest. Take a break. Relax. Don't let your fatigue cause you to overreact.

Fight Fair

Let's face it, in any relationship (even the perfect marriage), silly arguments and meaningless conflicts will arise. Living

Rested and Ready

Question: "What one piece of advice would you give parents who are about to have a teenager living in their home?"

Answer: "I'd tell them to clear their schedules because they're going to need all the time and energy possible. They will need to be rested and ready."

—Gail Veerman

with people always brings some friction. At times, especially when we're tired or dealing with our own problems, we over-react, causing the conflict to escalate. This process may continue until a full-blown, knock-down-drag-out argument ensues with the original (and small) irritation long forgotten. When this occurs, we need to remember to fight fair at all costs, even when we are livid or dealing with truly important issues.

"Unfair" fighting involves hitting people where they are vulnerable, where it hurts the most. This can include ridiculing a physical characteristic, bringing up an emotional weakness or information that was given in confidence, or reexamining a past sin or indiscretion. A husband might say, "You're just like your mother!" or "Oh yeah, well with those extra pounds, you're no prize!" A wife might shout, "Now I can see why you got passed over for that promotion at work!" or "If you were a better father, you'd know why your son is hurting right now." Or a parent might respond to a teenager with, "No wonder you don't have any friends!" or "You can be such a jerk!" or "Last year you were accused of cheating—maybe it was true after all!"

Comments like those are unfair. Not only do they inflict serious harm, but we will also later regret having said them.

No matter how serious the violation, there is no place in loving relationships for name-calling or insults, especially those that strike at the heart of a person's identity. So in our battles with our teenagers, we need to fight fair, quietly describing our feelings and firmly and calmly explaining our positions and their implications. For example, "You know that you shouldn't talk to your mother like that. And you know the consequences . . ." or "What you did makes me very upset. In fact, I'm furious. I'm also very disappointed because I expect better of you!" or "I'm so angry right now that I'm afraid I will say something that I shouldn't and will regret later. So go to your room, and we'll discuss this in an hour when I've had time to collect my thoughts."

Notice that in all of those examples, the mother or father focused on the offending action, not on the person, and, for the most part, used "I" words rather than "you" accusations. The parent described his or her feelings (including anger), along with the reasons for those feelings, and then moved on, without swearing or calling names. That's fighting fair. Remember, "A gentle answer turns away wrath, but harsh words stir up anger" (Prov. 15:1 NLT).

Don't Withhold Emotional Support

When the going gets rough, some parents withdraw from their teenagers emotionally. They distance themselves from their kids by not giving them encouragement, love, or support. Sometimes this can be worse for children than physical punishment. When times get tough, teenagers need emotional support. They can survive without their parents' money or advice, but they don't do well without their love. And if they don't get this love and support at home, they are likely to look for it elsewhere.

> In matters of principle, stand like a rock. In matters of taste, swim with the current.
>
> —Thomas Jefferson

Whether our teens mess up a little or a lot, or just hurt our feelings, we shouldn't withhold hugs and other signs of affirmation or affection. Some parents respond with the silent treatment, avoiding and ignoring the offending teenager entirely. But that's a mistake and is always counterproductive. In any conflict, we need to talk it out. And no matter what the cause or outcome, we should always let our kids know we are glad they are ours. This includes smiling when we see them and affirming them when possible. When kids know that Mom and Dad are on their side, they will be able to handle the tough times.

Remember, Kids Aren't Perfect

We should forget about our children being the absolute best and shouldn't expect them to live up to our unrealistic standards. If we judge our success as a parent by whether our kids turn out perfectly, we will be setting ourselves up for big-time failure because it will never happen. Instead, we should accept our children, especially our teenagers, for who they are, recognizing that they, just like us, are in process. If we accept their imperfections, we will probably have fewer battles to fight.

On Your Team

I have seen parents fight battles over nonessentials such as the purchase of a first bra for a flat-chested premenstrual adolescent girl. For goodness sake! If she wants it that badly, she probably needs it for social reasons. Run, don't walk, to the nearest department store and buy her a bra. The objective . . . is to keep your kids on your team. Don't throw away your friendship over behavior that has no moral significance. There will be plenty of real issues that require you to stand like a rock. Save your big guns for those crucial confrontations.

James Dobson, *Parenting Isn't for Cowards* (Dallas, TX: Word, 1987), 153.

Remember, We're Not Perfect Either

Have you ever scolded one of your children for spilling something on the carpet only to spill something yourself five minutes later? Chances are good you have been guilty of leaving your dirty socks in the middle of the floor, forgetting to close the refrigerator door, using unacceptable language, or being too tired to do a chore. If we remember that we're not perfect, we will be able to respond to our teenagers with more grace.

Apologize When Necessary

Certainly occasions will arise when we will unleash our anger on our teenagers only to discover later that the overreaction was unwarranted. We may even discover that we were wrong. We may find out that the teenager was telling the truth after all, that someone else was to blame, or that we simply misunderstood the situation. At these times, we owe our teenagers apologies. This is much easier said than done. It can be very difficult because pride gets in the way. Some parents think that apologizing means showing weakness, but the opposite is true. Nothing communicates love and integrity to a teenager better than a person, especially Mom or Dad, asking for forgiveness. It's good to say, "I was wrong. Will you forgive me?"

Remember: This Too Shall Pass

When we are going through tough circumstances, there may be reasons for concern or intervention. But many situations will take care of themselves if we just give them some time. For example, if a teenager is having problems with schoolwork, it may not be the end of the world. And he'll probably do better after the football season. Or, if you don't like the way your daughter dresses right now, wait until she leaves home and gets a job. She'll suddenly become Ms. Fashion.

Most of these minor irritations have a way of working themselves out over time if we can keep a long-term perspective.

So let's think again—what issues cause the blowups? What habits drive you crazy? What annoying actions get under the skin? Ignore them. Let them go. Relax. Pick your battles wisely, or you'll be battling all the time.

THINK IT THROUGH

1. Which of the scenes at the beginning of the chapter sound like your home during your teenage years?
2. On a scale of one to five, how would you rate your parents regarding their strictness, with one being very permissive and five being very strict? Why? Where would you put yourself on this continuum? Why?

3. What evidence do you see that you are a perfectionist? How has that tendency affected your relationships with your teenagers?

4. On what issues should you "loosen your grip"? On which ones should you tighten it?

5. What are your "hot buttons"? What can you do to "insulate" them?

6. What are some unfair weapons that you have used in an argument recently? What unfair weapons have been used against you by your teenagers?

7. When did you last use the silent treatment in a conflict? What was the result? How could you have better resolved the conflict?

8. Why is it difficult for you to admit to your teenagers that you were wrong? For what do you need to ask forgiveness as soon as possible?

Break the "No-Talk" Rule before It Breaks Your Family

A little boy had to write a report for school, so he went to his mother and asked, "Mom, where did I come from?"

Surprised at such a question from her child, the mother discreetly answered, "Um, the stork brought you."

"And where did *you* come from?" the boy continued.

"Well, the stork brought me, just like he brought you. Now go to your room. No more questions, please."

But the boy persisted. "What about Grandma? Where did Grandma come from?"

"Look, the stork brought Grandma, the stork brought me, the stork brought you! Now go to your room; I do not want to talk about this anymore!"

So the little boy went to his room and began writing his report: "Our family hasn't had a normal birth in three genera- tions. . . ."

It's a humorous story that maybe you've heard before, but it illustrates a fact—parents often feel awkward and frustrated when discussing sex with their children.

Actually, parents have a hard time discussing many thorny issues with their kids: ethics, the future, self-image, politics, money, faith, time, and death, just to name a few. But undoubt- edly the most difficult topics are sexuality and substance abuse (illegal drugs, alcohol, and tobacco). When these issues arise with teenagers because of an incident in the school or com- munity, a situation in a television show or a movie, or an out- right question, we probably don't answer with "the stork brought you" or something similar. Instead, we may try the silent approach and ignore the issue or, perhaps, change the subject.

THE NEED TO TALK

While these topics make most parents feel very uncomfort- able, our children must learn about them. In the absence of information or the presence of wrong information, lives can be shattered.

Our kids need to know the facts about sex, alcohol, and drugs. Even more important, they need to know what we, their parents whom they respect and love, think and believe—what our convictions and values are. However, many parents remain silent.

Why? Why is it so difficult to talk to our kids about drugs, alcohol, and sex? Why are no facts shared or beliefs expressed? Why do many teenagers have only a vague idea of how their parents feel about these issues? Here are just a few of the reasons some parents give for keeping the no-talk rule in place.

"If I talk about things like drugs and sex, that will only encourage my teenagers to try these things. It will make them more curious."

This is absolutely not true. Teenagers don't experiment with sex and drugs because they have information but because they are seeking it. They experiment with risky behaviors as a way of finding out for themselves what the fuss is all about. Kids are already curious. They have questions galore that need honest answers. Research has shown that if we talk it out, our kids will be much less likely to act it out.

"Only bad kids get involved with sex and drugs. If I talk to my teenagers about those things, they'll think I don't trust them."

While it's right to always communicate trust and respect to our teenagers, it's wrong to assume that only bad kids need to talk with their parents about sex and drugs. All kids need to know that their parents care enough about them to make sure they know the truth about these issues. We can have conversations with our teenagers in a manner that communicates love and respect rather than distrust.

"My teenagers already know everything."

Some parents think because their kids have sex or drug education at school or discuss these topics in the church youth group or see movies and television shows concerning them that little more needs to be said. While it is true that children and youth are being exposed to much more information today than in the past, the fact remains that they need to hear what their *parents* believe.

Are you comfortable with what your kids are learning outside the home or from the media about sexuality? Are you confident that your children understand why it's wrong to use drugs? Most kids hear very mixed messages from school, friends, the media—even from church. Unless you are willing to talk directly and frequently to your kids about sex and drugs, you can't be certain that they know what they need to know.

"My kids are too young."

Many parents wait . . . and wait . . . until they believe that their children are "old enough" to handle the information responsibly. In most cases, however, they wait too long. As we discussed in chapter 1, children growing up in today's world are bombarded with information about adult issues, usually without much in the way of explanation or guidance. Kids learn most of their information about sex, for example, from other children and the entertainment industry. They hear jokes about sex on TV sitcoms but don't understand why the jokes are so funny. They hear warnings about "safe sex" but aren't sure how it got to be so dangerous. How can you get hurt by kissing someone? Children have all sorts of questions they feel uncomfortable asking, and wise parents take the initiative to open up the communication lines *early*. Kids need to know that they can bring their questions to Mom or Dad and get straight, honest answers. Obviously there are some facts young children don't need to know, but generally it's best to start teaching our kids the truth about sex and drugs as soon as they are old enough to start asking questions.

"It's out of my comfort zone."

This is often said about sex. For many parents, sex is an awkward and embarrassing topic. It's difficult for many people to talk about it without giggling, blushing, or breaking into a cold sweat.

Your kids may be as embarrassed as you are, but sex has definitely come out of the closet in the last few years. It's the subject of almost every television show (including the evening news), and it finds its way into almost every conversation at school, work, and play. Today's kids may find it strange that the only place where people are afraid to talk about sex is at home.

Overheard on the Playground

Jimmy and Johnny are both five years old.

Jimmy: "Guess what? I found a condom out on the patio!"

Johnny: "Really? What's a . . . patio?"

Feeling uncomfortable with talking about sex is normal and OK. But we need to overcome those feelings and be honest with our kids, letting them know that we love them and want to make sure they get the truth.

"I don't know enough. I'll look stupid."

This statement usually refers to talking about drugs. It may be true that we are not experts on specific drugs and drug abuse, especially if we have no personal experience with them. But we still should share our beliefs and feelings with our children.

A recent TV campaign emphasizes this truth very well. In creative ads, parents are urged to talk to their kids about drugs, even if they look extremely foolish doing so. The message is that the conversation itself is important; that is, the fact that we are talking about drugs is more important than the specifics of our talks.

"I was no angel when I was a kid."

Some parents are reluctant to talk about sex or drugs and

alcohol with their children because they are afraid their kids will ask questions such as "Did you smoke marijuana when you were a teenager?" or "Were you a virgin when you got married?" These parents fear that if they answer truthfully about their teenage mistakes, they will give their kids justification for making the same mistakes.

Obviously, it's easier to teach abstinence or moral purity from a position of strength, but moral perfection is not required in order to have moral authority. If perfect parents are the only ones qualified to teach their kids right from wrong, then no one is qualified. Teenagers need to understand that although their parents aren't perfect, they are still trustworthy.

It is not necessary or advisable to reveal all of our past misdeeds to our children, and we shouldn't feel pressured to do so. What *we* did as teenagers is not the issue. Instead, the issue is what is right and what is wrong. Each individual is responsible for his or her own behavior. We should reveal only what will help our children make good choices for themselves. If you can use your experience to teach and motivate your kids to make good choices, then by all means do so. But don't let guilt stop you from talking with them. You will have to be sensitive to how much you should reveal. It's all right to let children know that you made mistakes as you were growing up, without revealing all the gory details.

If you think that your teenager will eventually learn the truth about your "sordid past" (for example, as a teenager, you had a child that you gave up for adoption; you are a recovering alcoholic; you spent time in prison for a drug-related offense; and so forth), then look for an opportunity to confess to your older children what you did and explain the lessons you learned from those wayward moments and bad choices. It's better for your kids to hear it from you, sooner, than from someone else, later. Be sure to bathe that conversation in prayer and to choose the right time and place.

"My parents never talked to me about sex and drugs, and I survived." In today's open society, when everyone is exposed to so much information and stimulation from every direction, we really can't afford to be evasive or apprehensive about discussing these important topics with our kids. If we don't break the no-talk rule now, it will break our families later.

A Teachable Moment Gone Awry

Johnny came home from school with a question for his mother. "What's sex?" asked the boy innocently.

Oh my, thought his mother. *It's here. The time has finally come for me to explain the birds and bees to my child. Oh, I wish his father were here; he could do this better. It's his responsibility. But I really shouldn't ignore the question. That would be wrong.*

So the mother sat little Johnny down, gave him some milk and cookies, and began to describe the human reproductive process in great detail while the young boy listened intently.

Finally, when she was finished, she asked Johnny, "Do you have any questions?"

"Well, just one. How am I going to put all that on my soccer team application where it says, 'Sex: M or F?'"

The irony in all of this is that these vulnerable spots are where popular culture through the media attacks young people today. For example, the most creative advertisements on television are for beer, and many ads use sexual innuendos to sell their products.

Certainly we find coarse jokes and bed scenes on TV and in films offensive, but even more destructive are the values being presented. Sex, for example, is pictured as life's cure-all. The prevailing philosophy of life seems to be: For meaning, purpose, and happiness, just have sex! And sexual play and intercourse are pictured as activities that a person does almost as casually as choosing fast food.

In our society, sex is *overrated* and *undervalued*. It is overrated in the sense that sex, while pleasurable, is not the *ultimate* pleasure that will bring meaning to life. As you walk through a mall, commute to the city, or fly on a commercial airline, look at the adults around you. The chances are good that most of them had sexual intercourse during the last fourteen days. Then consider this: How many of them look totally happy and fulfilled, especially if you see them in the morning? Most probably look worried, tired, frustrated, annoyed or angry, and bored.

Sex is undervalued in the sense that it is cheapened. While God created sex to be pleasurable, he also designed it to be enjoyed in the context of marriage, where husband and wife "become one" (see Gen. 2:23–25 and Mark 10:6–9). Sexual intercourse is the most intimate of experiences between a man and a woman—through it they become bonded emotionally and spiritually, as well as physically. In addition, one of the important purposes of sex is procreation, producing God-imaged human beings. According to the Bible and common sense, sex should be valued. Bed hopping, sex without commitment, abortion, and other popular contemporary behaviors are irresponsible, self-centered, and defiant acts.

Having examined the need and the problem, let's look at the

solution. First, here are some facts to help us understand the issues.

FACTS ABOUT SUBSTANCE ABUSE

Substance abuse is a huge problem among the population in general, so we shouldn't be surprised that teenagers are especially vulnerable both to experimentation and addiction. Unfortunately, for some teens, drinking or doing drugs has become a rite of passage that marks their entry into adulthood.

Alcohol

Americans love to drink alcohol (more than one hundred billion dollars' worth every year). If we want to have fun, we are told every day, have a beer or serve up a cocktail.

Alcohol is the most abused drug in North America, and beer is the alcoholic beverage of choice for most people, including teenagers. According to researchers, the average age for a "first drink" is 13.1 years, and the trend continues to move down to younger and younger children. Many teenagers report that they started drinking when they were in the fourth or fifth grade.

For most teenagers, alcohol is easy to get. If they can't get it at home, they get it from older friends, or they just buy it themselves. Fake ID's are a common teen accessory, and many stores that sell alcohol don't bother to check the age of the buyer. Some parents even encourage their teenage children to drink with the mistaken belief that alcohol is less dangerous than hard drugs. Or they assume that their teenagers will drink anyway, so they give them a safe place to drink—at home, under their supervision.

The truth is that alcohol abuse stands as the leading killer of adolescents. One-fourth of all accidents that result in teenage fatalities involve drunk driving. Alcohol also plays a major role in other risky behaviors common among teens, such as sexual promiscuity and criminal behavior—and it is the primary gateway to more serious drug abuse. According to researchers, teens who drink are 7.5 times more likely to abuse hard drugs.[1]

Drugs

It's no secret that North America continues to struggle with drug abuse. Despite much publicized "wars on drugs," there is no indication that this problem will disappear anytime soon. Actually, we live in a drug-dependent society—we have pills to remedy almost every ailment under the sun, including depression and sexual impotence. If we aren't feeling well or need an escape, we can take a drug that will solve our problem. Messages like these are well understood by today's kids.

According to researchers, more than half of all teenagers will use illegal drugs at least once before they graduate from high school. Sadly, most parents are completely unaware of their child's drug use, and others deny the obvious evidence.[2]

Drugs commonly used by teens include a wide variety of depressants, narcotics (such as opium and heroin), "designer drugs" ("Ecstasy" is the most popular), inhalants (glues, household cleaners, nitrous oxide or "laughing gas"), steroids, cocaine (including "crack"), stimulants like crystal meth and "ice," and, of course, marijuana. Parents are wise to acquaint themselves with these and other drugs that are widely available. Most have street names that describe the various forms in which these drugs can be found.

Young people start using drugs for many reasons. Some may try drugs because they perceive that it's a very grown-up thing to do. They watch adults (including entertainment and sports heroes) use and abuse drugs, and they feel compelled to imitate this behavior. Other factors include curiosity and experimentation, peer pressure, pop-culture and media glamorization of drugs, and family problems.

Many kids will do drugs simply to escape their problems because drugs seem like an easy way out.

Tobacco

While tobacco is generally considered less dangerous than alcohol and illegal drugs, the health risks involved in smoking cigarettes are well documented. Every year, the tobacco industry spends more than six billion dollars to advertise cigarettes and "smokeless" tobacco, and, despite claims to the contrary, most of that advertising is aimed at young people. The ad industry is well aware that if it can create brand loyalty when a person is young, it has that person for life. Make no mistake: The tobacco industry is targeting your kids. Its economic survival depends on them. It needs six million new smokers every day just to maintain current sales levels, and research has confirmed that 80 percent of all adult smokers took their first puffs while they were teens.

Besides the obvious health risks associated with smoking and other forms of tobacco use, we must remember that tobacco is yet another way teenagers enter the world of serious drug abuse. Studies have found that teenage smokers are 23 times more likely to use marijuana, 12 times more likely to use heroin, and 51 times more likely to use cocaine.

FACTS ABOUT TEENAGE SEXUALITY

Teenagers are sexually active. They may not necessarily be "having sex," but they are most definitely sexually active. The onset of puberty marks the beginning of a lifetime of sexual maturity, sexual awareness, and sexual activity that includes everything from sexual fantasies to sexual intercourse. Early adolescent boys and girls must come to terms with a variety of sexual feelings that are variously exciting, puzzling, and frightening.

While today's teenagers are certainly no different from previous generations in this regard, they are unique in that they are growing up in a culture that both exploits sex and eschews moral responsibility. The sexual revolution of the 1960s left behind a moral ambivalence that is very confusing to children and teenagers. Many young people have no idea what is right and wrong when it comes to sexual behavior.

According to research from the U.S. Centers for Disease Control, 37 percent of ninth graders have had sexual intercourse, 48 percent of tenth graders, 59 percent of eleventh graders, and 67 percent of high school seniors. The average age for first-time sexual intercourse is reported to be fifteen for girls and fourteen for boys.[3]

Where do kids begin experimenting with sex? You might be surprised to learn that more than half of all teens who have had sex say they had their first sexual encounter *at home*, usually, but not always, when their parents were away.

For many teenagers at the turn of the millennium, sex has simply become a normal and accepted part of growing up. It's everywhere—not only in the popular entertainment but also on the evening news. It's not surprising that some teenagers feel abnormal because they are sexually inexperienced. As one fifteen-year-old girl put it, "I had sex just to get it over with."

The consequences of sexual promiscuity among teenagers have increased in recent years as well. Besides the spiritual and emotional consequences of guilt and heartache, there is the danger of an unwanted pregnancy. Most sexually active teenagers use neither condoms nor other birth-control methods. More than a million teenage girls in the United States become pregnant every year, and it is estimated that 40 percent of today's fourteen-year-old girls will become pregnant at least once before they reach the age of twenty. One tragic consequence of this has been the enormous increase in abortions performed on teenage girls since the 1973 *Roe v. Wade* decision.

Another consequence of greater sexual activity among teens is the increased spread of sexually transmitted diseases, or STD's. A generation or two ago, we were familiar with only three STD's (what was then called VD or venereal disease). Today there are more than thirty, including chlamydia, gonorrhea, syphilis, HPV (or genital warts, which the Centers for Disease Control says may infect up to 40 percent of all teenage girls in the United States), herpes (several kinds), pelvic inflammatory disease (PID, which infects more than 200,000 teenage girls every year), and, of course, AIDS.[4]

WHAT TO DO

Faced with media assault and cultural pressure, we can feel almost helpless, as though the battle has already been lost. But that's not true. We can make a difference, *if we take action and talk*.

Talk Early

Obviously, it's best to start when our children are young. One reason why it's so difficult for some parents to talk to their teenagers about sensitive issues like sex and drugs is because they never have. If we can let kids know early that these issues

More than the Birds and the Bees

Do you find it difficult to talk to your teenagers about sex? Do your kids shy away from asking you questions about sexual matters? You're not alone. Most young people have difficulty asking their parents about sexuality—and many parents feel uncomfortable talking with their kids about the topic.

It's not easy to talk with adolescents about sex. But if you are willing to break the "no-talk" rule, you will not only help your teenagers understand the truth about sex, but you'll also communicate that you care. It is important to let kids know that you are approachable and unshockable. You can do this by conversing with your teenagers in a nonthreatening, comfortable climate. Use the following suggestions to help you in your communication.

Teach them what you believe. They really do want to know. They need to know your values, convictions, and moral stands. Share your beliefs about dating, petting, premarital sex, marriage, and the family. Help dissolve the myths they've learned about sex from the popular media. Discuss not only values and information, but also feelings. Ask them how they feel about their bodies, about themselves, about love. Use examples from your own adolescent past. Discuss how you felt when you fell in love, dated, and got married.

Ask them questions, especially if they're having problems sharing with you. Use opportunities such as TV shows that deal with sexual issues to open dialogue. Avoid asking personal questions of a sexual nature ("What did you do with your date last Friday night?"). Instead, ask their opinions on general topics such as love, relationships, dating, birth control, venereal disease, sexual values, or what the school is teaching about sexuality. If your teenager doesn't want to talk, don't give up. Wait for another time, but keep asking those questions lovingly and gently. You can do it.

Listen to what your adolescents have to say. When they do ask questions, don't brush them off. If you don't have time at the moment to answer, make a date for a later time to discuss their concerns. Reinforce their questions with affirming responses like "I remember asking that question" or "That's a good question." This builds trust into your relationship. Affirming responses show your children that you care and that it's OK to ask questions. Don't be afraid if you can't answer every question. None of us can answer everything, especially when it comes to sex.

Kindle a desire in your teenagers to ask your opinion. This means being warm and understanding. It means realizing that your kids are sexual beings with sexual desires. It means accepting them for who they are, not for what they've done. It means keeping their questions confidential, rather than sharing the intimacies of their lives with their siblings, relatives, or friends. It means trying to influence your children rather than trying to manipulate, control, or overpower them. It means taking time out of your day to share concerns, hurts, and problems. It means providing a nonthreatening, trusting environment in which to communicate.

are not off-limits or too embarrassing to be discussed with their parents, the communication lines will be open when we want to talk later.

What do we talk about? With younger children, our conversations about sex should be age-appropriate, of course. Resources are available to help with this, but the most important thing to remember is that kids have questions and are seeking satisfactory answers. It's easy for children to arrive at many wrong conclusions about sex and drugs based on the bits and pieces of information (or misinformation) they pick up from advertisements, TV shows, comedians, writing on the bathroom wall, friends, school, and elsewhere. They need to know that the best place to get the truth about all this puzzling information is Mom or Dad. Certainly, we don't want to dump more information on kids than they can handle, but if we let them know at an early age that we are approachable and willing to talk, we will be in a better position to do so when they are teenagers.

Talk Often

We should remember that it takes more than "The Talk." In the past, parents often waited until their children were a certain age and then gave them "The Talk" about sex. Every parent had a responsibility to let each child know about "the birds and the bees." But once parents had given kids "The Talk," they were finished. From that point on, young people were on their own.

Today, some parents take essentially the same approach. Whether the topic is sex, drugs, or any other important issue, they mistakenly think that once they have given their kids an appropriate lecture, they have done their duty.

It's best to think of breaking the no-talk rule as "continuing education"—talks rather than "The Talk." It should be an ongoing dialogue throughout the teen years. Obviously, this will be much easier for parents who are able to discuss other matters with their kids—who have opened the lines of communication.

Take Advantage of Teachable Moments

The best way to talk to kids about issues such as sex and drugs is to do it naturally. Rather than calling a special meeting

Kids Want "Supersized" Talks on Life

A new national survey [released March 1, 1999] found that while parents are talking to their kids about AIDS, sex, alcohol, and drugs, it's often not early enough or in-depth enough for what their children expect. The "big talk," said one youth activist, needs to be "supersized" to deal with issues like peer pressure to have sex and how alcohol and drugs might affect decisions to have sex. If parents don't step in, the survey found, kids end up relying on friends, television, movies, and, more recently, the Internet.

The good news for parents, the survey sponsors said, is that their kids want their advice on those tough issues. And parents of pre-teens are talking about the basics: 90 percent have talked about drugs/alcohol, 78 percent about AIDS, and 73 percent about how girls get pregnant. The bad news is that the basics aren't enough, and a gap exists between what parents talk about and what kids want to know.

From a report on MSNBC (http://www.msnbc.com/news/245543.asp).

at a special time, we should wait for opportunities and openings to ask questions, share our opinions, offer advice. We shouldn't try to make *every moment* a teachable one, but times will arise when the subject is ripe for discussion. Then we can seize the moment and talk.

How do you respond when you are watching television with your children and the dialogue or the action turns to sex? What do you do? Some parents grab the TV remote and change channels. Others hope their children aren't paying attention. (They are.) But smart parents will talk over the TV, initiating a conversation right then and there, while the program is still on. Why should the TV do all the talking? Kids need to learn how to think, and one of the best ways to teach them is to think out loud in front of them. This will also help them learn to think as Christians.

We can also discuss movies after seeing them (we aren't supposed to talk in the theater). Whenever we have the opportunity to share our values and faith with our kids, we should do it. Take advantage of teachable moments.

Do Homework

Take the time to become better informed about such topics as sex and drugs. We don't have to become experts on these things, but if we show an interest and get the facts before having discussions with our teens, we will send the message that these things matter to us. Parents who aren't willing to take the time to read a book, look up information on the Internet, or attend a seminar communicate just the opposite—that they don't care.

When discussing the biblical view of sex, for example, we should be sure to do our own Bible study to find out exactly what the Bible teaches. We can read and study passages such as Genesis 1:27–28; 2:18–25; 2 Samuel 13:1–20; Proverbs 5; 6:23–25; Song of Songs 4:1–16; Matthew 5:27–30; Romans 6:1–14; 1 Corinthians 3:19–20; 6:9–7:9; Ephesians 5:1–3; Colossians 3:5; 1 Thessalonians 4:1–8; Hebrews 13:4; 2 Peter 3:14.

We need to help our kids understand that God's Word has a very high view of sex. It is most definitely one of God's best ideas and is in no way dirty or illicit. God invented sex to be enjoyed for a lifetime by husbands and wives together, to express love to each other, and to have children. God has many good reasons for condemning fornication, adultery, homosexuality, and other forms of promiscuity. God's guidelines about sex don't result from some divine desire to take all the fun out of life. Instead, he wants us to enjoy life to its fullest (see John 10:10).

Can you explain these ideas to your kids? If not, do your homework and learn how to communicate God's truth. Don't leave it to the church or to someone else.

Similarly, it would be wise to learn important facts about sexually transmitted diseases and drugs so that we can discuss them intelligently with our kids. Again, we don't have to become experts in these areas, but we can learn about the most common STD's and how they are transmitted and treated. We can learn about the most common drugs and how to identify signs that our teenagers may be involved. Excellent resources such as Walt Mueller's *Understanding Today's Youth Culture* provide many facts and figures worth discussing with kids.

Why Sex?

Contrary to popular opinion, most young people engage in sexual activity for psychological rather than hormonal reasons. If teenagers feel secure, loved, and appreciated at home, they are not likely to seek comfort and support elsewhere in the form of premature sexual intimacy.

David Elkind, *Parenting Your Teenager* (New York: Ballantine Books, 1993), 73.

Don't Be Afraid to Get Help

Parents who are able to talk with their teenagers about sex and drugs or who know for certain that their teenagers are abusing drugs, having sex, or engaging in other forms of risky behavior should seek professional help. They should contact a pastor, a family counselor, or anyone they know who might be able to give helpful counsel and resources for intervention. The worst option is to do nothing. Caring parents will do whatever it takes to make sure that their teenagers don't end up hurting themselves or anyone else through their irresponsible behavior.

Add an Ounce of Prevention

We should remember that most teenagers who gravitate toward risky behaviors do so because they lack something important in their lives. Some teens try drugs because they are bored or depressed or have low self-esteem. A large number of teens become sexually promiscuous because they want love and affection and have come to believe that sex is the best way to get it. Emotionally healthy teenagers, however, are much less inclined to participate in behaviors that are self-destructive. It's important to talk with our kids about sex and drugs; it's even more important to stay connected to them, treat them with respect, and let them know how much we love and appreciate them.

A recent federally funded study of teenagers (costing more than twenty-five million dollars) concluded that "teens who have a strong sense of connection to their parents are less likely to be violent or indulge in drugs, alcohol, tobacco, or early sex."[5] This, the study found, is true all the way through high school. We can make a difference.

Let's not give in or give up. Instead, let us commit to breaking the no-talk rule before it breaks our families.

THINK IT THROUGH

1. What topics do you find difficult to discuss with your teenagers? Why?

2. What excuses have you used for avoiding talking with your teenagers about sexuality and substance abuse?

3. In which of these areas do you feel unqualified to talk to your teenagers: sex, drugs, alcohol, tobacco?

4. How has drug usage in your community changed since you were a teenager? How does this affect the need for drug education?

5. From whom did you learn about sex? When did you have "The Talk" with your parent(s)? What do you remember from that discussion?

6. When did you begin to talk with your children about sex? About drugs? About alcohol? About tobacco? If you haven't started yet, when will you?

7. How do you recognize a teachable moment? How have you taken advantage of those moments in the past?

8. Where can you find helpful information about drugs and alcohol? About sex?

9. If you had a serious sex-, drug-, or alcohol-related problem in your home, where could you find help?

10. What can you do to make your home more talk-friendly regarding these important issues?

Chapter 11

Don't Handicap Teenagers by Making Life Too Easy for Them

- A cry shatters the night, and Mommy runs to the crib to hold the baby, soothe her feelings, and rock her back to sleep.
- Careening down the driveway, little Bradley tries to negotiate a quick turn with his Big Wheel onto the sidewalk. His forward momentum wins, however, tipping the Big Wheel and sending Bradley sprawling. Witnessing the accident from the front porch, Daddy jumps down the stairs and dashes to his son, comforting him and assuring him that everything will be all right.
- At dinner, Melody tells with frustration and anger of another fourth-grade girl who has been teasing her

mercilessly. Dad listens intently and decides to give Melody's teacher a call.

- While running after a loose soccer ball, Jordan is inadvertently tripped by an opponent. He lies on the field, obviously in pain, clutching his ankle. Along with the coach, Jordan's mother rushes to his side.

- The spring day had started so gloriously—bright sun, warm breeze, and plenty of fun activities. But a phone call shatters the mood and the family as word comes of Grandpa's fatal heart attack. Then through their own tears, Mom and Dad pull the children close and tell them about heaven.

In each of these situations, the parent or parents are acting rightly, doing what they should. They love their children and know that it's their job to protect and heal and serve. They're good parents who want the very best for their kids.

That's why the thrust of this chapter is so difficult for most parents. We don't want to see our children get hurt or suffer in any way. Thus, we try to make life as painless for them as we possibly can.

That's fine when they are children, of course. What parent wouldn't run barefoot over broken glass to rescue his or her child from danger or pain? When children are small, we do everything for them, from changing their diapers to getting them dressed in the morning. We can hardly do enough for infants and toddlers.

What many parents don't realize, however, is that when their offspring become teenagers, they aren't children anymore. They are *young adults in training*. Thus, as discussed in chapter 5, they need to be equipping themselves for adulthood, developing the skills necessary to become capable and self-reliant adults, and learning how to become responsible and how to take care of themselves. Parents who make life too easy for their teenagers—always running to the rescue—interfere with this process and usually end up stunting the teenagers' growth.

Here are just a few of the ways that parents handicap their teens:

- Getting them out of bed in the morning, doing their laundry, fixing their lunches, and picking out their clothes
- Loaning them money, giving them extra money after they have spent their allowance, or letting them spend designated funds, such as a clothing allowance, on something else
- Buying them cars, stereos, TVs, toys, designer-label clothing, and other "essentials" whenever they want them
- Typing papers, doing research, delivering forgotten homework or lunches to school, and lying to teachers for them when they cut classes or skip school
- Bailing them out of trouble whenever they get into it, fixing their problems, and paying the penalty for their mistakes
- Feeling sorry for them when they have a lot of homework or extracurricular activities and excusing them from helping the family with household chores

None of these actions sound all that terrible, do they? In most cases, our motives for taking these actions are good. We just want to protect and help our kids, to give them everything they need. And in today's busy world, this is how many modern parents express love to their teenagers. Rather than spending quality time with them or developing quality relationships, they make the mistake of giving their kids too much. Of course, what teenager in his or her right mind wouldn't want to keep it that way?

Lessons

If I had just one day to live over, it would be the day the principal of Coral Gables High School called me and said, "Mr. Perkins, your son Steve has just been arrested for possession and sale of marijuana here on our school campus. The police are taking him to the Dade County jail."

I listened in disbelief as the principal continued. "Mr. Perkins, the reason I'm calling is that Steve's arrest is not only a legal problem, it is also a school problem. Steve is a marginal student. If he misses many days of school as a result of being in jail, it's likely that he'll fail his junior year here at Coral Gables High."

I listened numbly until I heard the principal's voice saying goodbye. Then I dropped the phone to the table. I could feel my desperation rising.

I loved my son; I couldn't let that happen; I couldn't let him fail. I immediately called an attorney and that afternoon we bailed Steve out of jail. Within a few days the attorney managed to get all of the charges against Steve dropped.

That was many years ago. Since then I've learned more about alcohol, other drugs, and kids. If I had to make that decision today, I would consider leaving my son in the Dade County jail. I say that because today I know children are always learning from parents—and my son learned two things from me the day I bailed him out of jail.

First, he learned I was a liar. I had told him if he didn't stop "messing around" with alcohol and other drugs, something bad would happen to him. But the first time something did happen, I stepped in and took away his opportunity to learn from the consequences of drug abuse. Steve learned that my words were empty. Nothing bad was going to happen as a result of his drug use.

My son learned a second lesson that day. He learned if he *did* use drugs and he did get into trouble, someone else would take responsibility for his decisions. Someone else would bail him out. Someone else would clean up the mess.

Sadly, he learned those lessons well. Steve continued to use drugs and find people who would insulate him from the problems caused by his drug use. He did that until, as he told me recently, he was almost dead.

Why didn't I leave my son in the Dade County jail? What stopped me from doing what I knew was best for my son? I've asked myself those questions many times over the years. I've found some answers, and some of those answers are difficult to admit, even to myself. I wish I could simply say, "I did it because I loved him." Certainly that's one of the reasons. But there are other reasons that don't have anything to do with love. They have to do with fear, pride, selfishness, and ego.

William Mack Perkins, *Raising Drug Free Kids in a Drug-Filled World* (New York: Harper & Row, 1986), 75–76.

LONG-RANGE PARENTING

But there's another reason we sometimes make life too easy for our teenagers: *to make life easy for us!* This works for the short-term because it gets immediate results. Problems are solved, work gets done, and no margin is left for error. When we do everything for our teenagers, the work will likely be done right the first time. When we give our kids what they want, we save ourselves from having to argue with them or convince them that they should wait for it or figure out how to get it on their own. Parents take this route because they simply don't have the time or the patience to do otherwise.

This may make life easier for parents, but it can be devastating in the long-term for kids, who later discover that life just doesn't work that way. People aren't going to give them everything they want whenever they want it. They aren't going to be able to manipulate the boss the way they did Mom and Dad, nor will they be able to continue sidestepping the consequences of their actions. Sooner or later, they will come to realize that they are ill-equipped to function responsibly in the real world.

That's why it's important to practice long-range parenting. Our ultimate goal as parents should be to help our children grow into capable, self-reliant adults. With that in mind, we need to ask in every situation, "What is the best way to help our teens become more responsible in the long-term?" Rarely will the answer be the best short-term solution. It will undoubtedly be the least painful way to get through the day, but this short-term solution may undermine teenagers' chances for success as adults.

THE VALUE OF CONSEQUENCES

We can begin practicing long-range parenting by allowing teens to experience the consequences of their actions whenever possible. The tendency for parents is to want to rescue—to provide an easy way out. But the only way kids will ever learn life skills such as responsibility, self-discipline, and good judgment is to understand the relationship between their actions and the results of those actions.

Self-Esteem

Most teenagers will try to avoid the consequences of their actions whenever possible, but consequences actually build self-esteem. They are good for teenagers! That's because consequences provide them with a very real sense of empowerment. Consequences establish a direct relationship between behaviors (what I do) and outcomes (what happens to me). Kids who experience consequences learn that they have power to control what happens in their lives. "I can make good things happen or I can make bad things happen. It's all up to me. I am in control of my life." That's a very freeing truth for a young person to learn.

On the other hand, young people who are considered most "at-risk" usually feel powerless and see themselves as victims. These kids grow up thinking that nothing is ever their fault and that things "just happen" to them. They believe in fate or luck and tend to blame everyone else for their problems or failures. If they flunk a test, for example, their natural impulse is to blame the teacher, their parents, or the school system—anyone but themselves. This kind of thinking likely comes from growing up in an environment with few consequences.

Discipline

Consequences are also the best way to discipline teenagers. Hardly any task of parenthood is more challenging than discipline. Most people equate it with punishment; in reality, the goal of discipline is to shape young people's character, to help them become more mature and independent. Discipline is not something that we do to teenagers; it is a way to help them learn to lead responsible, productive lives.

How do we discipline teenagers? Punishment is not very effective. Teens are, after all, too big to spank. So what do we do? Yelling and screaming are counterproductive and move the focus from the offense to our out-of-control response. And let's face it, some parents have grounded their kids so many times that the kids have gotten used to it and now accept grounding as a fact of life. Other kids rebel and simply don't care what their parents do to them anymore.

When children become teenagers, they want a new kind of relationship with their parents. If your relationship with your teen is generally negative, it doesn't have to stay that way. You and your teen can learn mutual respect. Teenage rebellion usually starts brewing when kids see themselves in a master-slave relationship with their parents. Adolescents are struggling to establish their own identities and want to be treated with dignity and respect. When they don't get it, they misbehave. Seeing this as a threat to their authority, many parents respond by clamping down even harder, leading to a vicious cycle of disrespect, disobedience, and discouragement.

To avoid that cycle, we need to learn to work with our teenagers rather than against them. Discipline is positive; punishment is not. If we learn how to discipline by using natural and logical consequences effectively, we can extinguish the fires of rebellion. We should think of discipline not as a way for us to be in control or in charge, but as a learning process for our kids. Our discipline can lead them to self-discipline and guide teens toward becoming responsible.

USING CONSEQUENCES EFFECTIVELY

There are two kinds of consequences—natural ones and logical ones. Depending on the situation, both are important ways for teenagers to learn responsibility and self-discipline.

Natural Consequences

A natural consequence is anything that happens naturally to a person, with no outside interference. If a person jumps out of a window, that person will go down. Someone standing in the rain will get wet. On a cold day, the person who doesn't wear a coat outside will get cold. Those who don't eat get hungry. Whoever touches a hot stove gets burned.

Children can learn a great deal about responsibility by experiencing natural consequences. Our tendency as parents, however, is to interfere—to rescue our children from natural consequences. We do this because we love our kids and want the best for them. After all, what parent feels good about allowing a child to be wet, cold, or hungry?

Remember the first time your child went off to school without his or her lunch? When you discovered the lunch on the kitchen counter, you probably began having visions of your child sitting forlornly at the lunch table, starving to death while all the other kids ate their lunches. So you jumped into the car, delivered the lunch, and saved the day! (By the way, research has found that it takes an average of sixty-five days to starve to death.)

We can get by with that for a while with small children. But when kids get older, rescuing becomes extremely counterproductive. For example, when we deliver a teen's forgotten lunch, we send that teenager the very clear message that he or she can go through life being forgetful and irresponsible and nothing bad will ever happen. People don't need to become responsible when somebody else will always fix things for them. Parents who insist on rescuing their adolescents from natural consequences should expect someday to have twenty-six-year-old teenagers living at home, still believing that Mom and Dad will take care of them, provide them with food and shelter, and cover for all their mistakes.

Consider how natural consequences would apply in the following situations:

- Your teenage son asks you for $10 to go out with friends. He forgot to budget money from his allowance for the weekend, but he really wants to spend some time with these friends. And they're really good kids.

In this situation, the natural consequence is almost anything other than giving him $10. It may be simply allowing him to take responsibility for the situation himself. He may want to find a way to earn the $10 (are there any odd jobs he can do?). He may ask for a loan (to be paid back with interest?) or an advance on next week's allowance. He may need to think of an activity that he and his friends can do together for free. Numerous options are available. Unfortunately, however, too many parents don't allow their kids to experience these consequences and learn. They just give the kid $10 because that's the easiest thing to do. The problem is solved, and it only cost ten bucks. But through this experience, the young man is learning that he doesn't have to be responsible. He has no need to budget.

- Your teenage daughter has a date and needs her green pants. She forgot to put them in the dirty clothes hamper earlier in the week, so they didn't get washed on the regular laundry day. She pleads with you to wash them now.

In this situation, let's assume that you are the parent who normally does the laundry for your family every week on specified laundry days. You have to constantly nag your daughter to pick up her dirty clothes off the floor and put them in the hamper, explaining that if she doesn't, they won't get washed. Now, since she failed to do so, the natural consequences are (a) wear the green pants dirty, (b) wear some other pants instead, or (c) do the laundry herself. All of these options are vastly superior to your doing a special laundry to stop your daughter from whining. After experiencing natural consequences like these a few times, she will learn to start putting her clothes in the hamper, and you will no longer have to nag.

- Your teenage son's grades have been slipping. He was an exceptional student until this year. Now, he's on the football team, active in several clubs, and dating a classmate. You are worried that he won't get into a good college. You've tried to get him to study harder, but your encouragement seems to be doing no good. Now, you are considering making him give up his extracurricular activities.

Letting teenagers work out their own school problems is one of the greatest challenges of parenting. It's not easy to sit on the sidelines and watch teenagers throw the future away by not performing up to their potential. Parents have a lot at stake. It's no wonder that for many parents and teens, schoolwork and grades are major causes of conflict.

In the above situation, intervention would only make things worse. Making the boy quit the football team would only lead to more conflict, more rebellion. Instead, Mom and Dad need to recognize that the problem belongs to the teen, not the parents. When parents let teenagers manage their own schoolwork, the first result is that conflict is reduced dramatically. And teens often learn to accept responsibility for their work when it ceases to be an issue between them and their parents. Because many teenagers use school performance as a weapon, they're literally disarmed when their parents step out of the conflict.

The goal is to get the teenager to take responsibility for his or her own school performance. In a situation like this, you could say, "Son, I've been on your back about schoolwork for a long time, and I've decided that it's no longer my problem. The responsibility for school belongs to you, so I won't check up on you anymore. I hope you do well, but it's up to you." When you take that approach, you have to be sure to mean what you say. Be prepared for your teenager to test you. Grades may drop for a while, and homework may go unfinished. That's how a teenager may try to tempt you to get involved again. But if you can resist interfering and simply encourage your teenager to do his or her best, you'll be surprised by how well he or she does.

- Your daughter gets a ticket for speeding. She tells you that the police officer singled her out and treated her unfairly. She bursts into tears. You consider calling the police station to file a complaint on her behalf.

It's normal for parents to want to stick up for their kids when they are feeling picked on or unfairly treated. "How dare they single out my daughter like that!" Sometimes we rescue because our pride has been ruffled, and we want to impress our kids with how tough or influential we can be. But it's wrong to fight our teenagers' battles for them.

In this situation, the daughter got a speeding ticket and probably deserved it. Just because she felt that she was treated unfairly doesn't change that fact. The best approach would be to listen empathetically and then encourage her to do whatever is necessary to remedy the situation. You could say, "Honey, I'm sorry that you felt the police officer singled you out. That must have been very frustrating. If you feel that he was being rude or unfair, then I suggest that you go down to the police department and file a complaint. If you don't believe that you are guilty of the speeding charge, you might consider going to court and pleading not guilty."

A good rule of thumb is to *never do for teenagers what they can do for themselves*. There are exceptions to this rule, of course, but they are rare. Teens need to learn how to take care of themselves, to solve their own problems. When teenagers get themselves into trouble, we have two options. We can send in the lifeboats, or we can teach them to swim. The first option will save them *this time*, but the second will save them *for a lifetime*. Kids who experience natural consequences tend to become good swimmers.

At times, however, natural consequences may be inappropriate, impractical, or ineffective, as when:

- *The consequence is too dangerous.* For example, if teenagers drink at a party, they should not be allowed to experience the "natural consequence" of putting themselves and others at risk by driving under the influence.
- *The consequence doesn't feel like a problem to the teenager.* For example, the natural consequence of not doing homework is bad grades. But for some teenagers, bad grades are not a problem.
- *There are no immediate natural consequences.* For example, there are no immediate natural consequences

for smoking a cigarette, failing to do chores, or breaking curfew. Those consequences tend to come later.

When any of these happen, it's time to switch to logical consequences.

Logical Consequences

Logical consequences don't happen naturally. They are set up by adults or by adults and teenagers together and agreed upon, if possible, in advance. They are logical because they are connected to the behavior in question.

Let's take curfew as an example. Your teenager is expected to be home by a certain time, let's say 11:00 P.M. What happens if he or she doesn't come home? You don't want the outcome to be left entirely up to you, which it will be if you don't have a logical consequence in place. You don't want to have to yell, scream, get mad, or unilaterally decree punishment on your teenager. So you decide with your teenager, in advance, on a logical consequence. This is reasonable. Explain to your teen that you will allow him or her to stay out until 11:00 P.M., but you need some assurance that he or she will be home at that time. (By the way, be sure to explain that "be home" means every part of the body in the house. Teenagers have been known to respond, "Oh, I thought you meant *start* home at eleven.") What will happen if the teenager fails to arrive home by the appointed time? (The consequence for parents is, of course, worry!) Most teenagers are reasonable enough to agree that having a consequence for this action would be appropriate. In fact, some teens are harder on themselves than their parents are! In any event, logical consequences are best when they are negotiated in advance with teenagers.

After the consequence has been agreed upon, you can pre-sent

Using Logical Consequences

- Decide if the problem is worth battling.
- Present consequences as choices. Choices within limits provide teenagers with opportunities to learn to make good decisions because *they* make the decision. ("Either come home at dinnertime or miss dinner"; "Either drive the speed limit, or I will drive"; "Either feed your dog, or we will give the dog away.")
- Consistently follow through if your teenager has chosen the consequence.
- Administer the consequence in a respectful rather than hostile, punitive manner. There is no need for lecturing, nagging, or gloating.
- Include your teenager in creating the consequence. Even if the teenager doesn't like it, he or she should understand the reason for it. Consequences are something you do *with* the teenager, not *to* the teenager.
- Separate your teenager from the behavior in question. One way is to change to a positive focus once the behavior and consequence are over.
- Never give a choice to your teenager that you could not follow through on. ("Either change your attitude or you can find another place to live!")

Remember—consequences are tools for teaching teenagers to be responsible for their actions and to make good choices for their lives. Consequences are not punishment, and they will fail if they are presented as such.

the teen's option as a choice that he or she alone will make. You can say, "Either be home by eleven o'clock or give up the right to use the car for the next month." When a teenager knows this in advance (and has agreed to it), then you are home free. You can relax. In the unlikely event that your teen does fail to come home by the appointed time, you still don't have to get angry. You can simply greet your son or daughter at the door and say something like, "I'm so relieved that you are safe. But I'm surprised that you have decided to stay home for the next month. I thought you enjoyed going out. But because you made this decision, I will make sure your wishes are granted. So give me the keys to the car." The teen may be upset, but he or she shouldn't be upset at you. After all, it's not your fault. You had nothing to do with him or her being grounded. In reality, the teenager grounded himself or herself.

Logical consequences should not be confused with punishment. Punishment is what parents do *to* kids, and it often leads to rebellion and broken relationships. But logical consequences involve the teenager in the process and are respectful.

In *Positive Discipline*, Jane Nelson describes what she calls "The Three Rs of Logical Consequences." These guidelines help ensure that solutions to problems are logical consequences and not punishment. The "Three Rs" are:

- Related
- Respectful
- Reasonable

According to Nelson, if any of the three Rs are missing from a solution, then it should no longer be considered a logical consequence.

For example, if a teenager tracks mud across the living room carpet, a logical consequence might require the teenager to clean the carpet. That consequence would be obviously *related* to the behavior in question. But what happens if either of the other Rs is missing?

Spoiled Consequences

Many attitudes and actions can undermine the effectiveness of logical consequences. Among them:

- *Being inconsistent.* Teens need to know what to expect. Try to be as consistent as possible (nobody's perfect).
- *Pitying.* Overprotective parents sometimes feel sorry for their teenagers and let them off the hook. Empathy is OK; pity is not.
- *Being overconcerned with what other people think.* Other people are not your kids' parents; you are.
- *Talking too much.* The purpose of logical consequences is to save your breath. Replace talk with action. Don't argue, just follow through.
- *Using inappropriate timing.* It's not a good idea to talk about consequences in the heat of battle. Either do it in advance or wait until emotions have calmed down.
- *Feeling and communicating hostility.* If your attitude is harsh or superior, your teen will regard the consequence as punishment.
- *Having hidden motives.* Logical consequences are not tricks to get your kids to do what you want. Nor are they a way to get even with your teen.
- *Playing detective.* When kids misbehave, do you conduct an investigation to find the true guilty party? In most families, that's impossible to do. Siblings like to blame each other and

deny responsibility. Put them all in the same boat and make them all accept the consequence. They can work it out, and it will discourage rivalry.

- *Rejecting the person instead of the act.* If you communicate that a bad act means the perpetrator is a bad person, your teen may feel hopeless. How can a bad person do *anything* good? A better response would be to say, "While I don't like what you've done, I still love you."

Adapted from Don Dinkmeyer and Gary D. McKay, *Parenting Teenagers: Systematic Training for Effective Parenting of Teens* (Circle Pines, MN: AGS, 1990), 129–32.

If the parent isn't *respectful* and adds humiliation or retribution to the requirement that the carpet be cleaned, then it is no longer a logical consequence. "Steve, how could you be so stupid! How many times do I have to tell you to leave your muddy shoes outside on the front porch! Now clean up the carpet or you'll be grounded for a month!" In this example, respect is eliminated and replaced with humiliation.

A logical consequence is *reasonable* when it is appropriate for the behavior in question—neither too much nor too little. If a parent were to make the teenager clean all the carpets in the house instead of just the one that he soiled, this would no longer be a logical consequence. Reasonableness would have been eliminated in favor of making the teenager suffer. Parents often do this because they believe that teens only learn from suffering. In most cases, however, unreasonable suffering inflicted on teens by parents only causes them to become bitter and rebellious.

In fact, says Nelson, when we eliminate any of the three Rs, our kids will likely experience the "Three Rs of Punishment," which are:

- Resentment ("This is unfair. I can't trust my parents.")
- Revenge ("They are winning now, but I will get even.")
- Rebellion ("Next time I won't get caught.")

To make logical consequences work with teenagers, the following process is advisable. First, discuss the situation with the teenager in a spirit of respect and mutual cooperation; next, brainstorm some possible solutions (logical consequences) that both parent and teenager can agree on. Then choose one and agree on a time frame or deadline if one is required (usually the case with things like chores, homework, or other responsibilities). When the deadline arrives, we don't have to get angry. We simply follow through on the agreement by holding the teenager accountable, with dignity and respect.

Teenagers will probably resist and test our resolve, but it's important to be tenacious and to avoid being manipulated. Remember, teens are very inventive and can often create dozens of great excuses and reasons why they should be let off the hook. That's why it's important to stay focused on the agreement and not let emotions take over. Teenagers need to learn that the real world operates by a system of laws and principles that cannot be manipulated by clever arguments or histrionics. The consistent application of logical consequences will help teens learn this lesson well.

Positive Consequences

Remember also that not all consequences have to be negative. Positive consequences can encourage positive behavior. Positive consequences come in the form of rewards. As with logical consequences, they, too, should be related, respectful, and reasonable.

Rewards should never be used as bribes. There is no reason to reward someone for doing something that he or she should be doing anyway. For example: Mr. McKinnon promised his teenage son Scott $5,000 upon graduation if he didn't use drugs in high school. The bribe didn't work, first, because Scott decided he didn't want his father's money, and second, because Scott's father communicated disrespect ("I don't trust you to stay off drugs on your own, so I'm bribing you").

Positive consequences should never be used that way. This is one of the reasons for not paying kids to do chores. If they are doing chores to get money, then they can decide not to do the chores whenever they don't need or want the money.

At times, teenagers should experience positive logical consequences. Real life doesn't exclude them. People who work hard for their employers all year will probably be rewarded with a raise, a promotion, or a bonus. While we shouldn't count on such rewards, the chances are good that doing what is right will lead to positive results. This isn't always the case, but it happens enough to motivate us to keep doing right.

If a teenage son sets aside his plans to hang out with friends in order to help clean the house before company arrives, he probably deserves a thank-you—not only verbally but perhaps with his parents' permission to go out with his friends that evening rather than stay home and help entertain the guests.

Keep in mind that in most cases, the best positive consequence for a teenager is a smile of appreciation, a word of encouragement, or a hug or handshake from Mom and Dad. We don't have to spend money or barter for our teens' good behavior. Sometimes a special gift or privilege will be deserved, but we need to remember the principle that heads this chapter: Don't handicap kids by making life too easy for them.

OVERINDULGENCE

Unfortunately, some parents handicap their kids by giving them way too much in the way of money, possessions, toys, clothes, and other material items. This is a common mistake because society is so materialistic. We are led to believe that happiness comes from lots of money and possessions even though, down deep, we know this is not true. It is also implied that love is expressed through buying the loved one expensive things. Merchandisers count on our believing this illusion.

One Gift Will Do

One thing I learned when my children were little is to never give your kids more than one gift at a time. If you give your child one gift, he or she will treasure it and enjoy it and be quite grateful for it. But if you bring your child *two* gifts, once the child has opened the second one, he or she will be disappointed that there isn't a third.

—Wayne Rice

Today's teenagers are often accused of being the most materialistic generation in history. If this is true, it's because we have made them that way by giving them too much, making life too easy for them, and presenting an unrealistic view of how the world works. Even though many parents preach the ethics of hard work, the same parents paradoxically undermine that message by giving to their kids excessively. Most children perceive behavior as reality—how a person acts means much more than what he or she says. Why work when you can have everything for free?

Cornucopia Kids

The cornucopia is the mythical horn of plenty always full to overflowing, the traditional symbol of a good harvest, a fitting sign of the good life in the suburbs. Children raised in this most comfortable environment experience the Cornucopia Complex—". . . the expectation, based on years of experience in the home, that the good life will always be available for the asking without effort and without the need for personal accountability."

In a nutshell, such children grow up with unrealistic expectations of the world of work they will have to face on their own, later. While in the home, there is little experience that leads to learning the direct relationship between effort and reward. Aided and abetted by unknowing parental conspirators, the work ethic in these children is slow to germinate and sometimes does not blossom at all.

Bruce Baldwin, *Beyond the Cornucopia Kids* (Wilmington, NC: Direction Dynamics, 1988), 18.

Children who have been victims of parental indulgence grow up believing that they are entitled to whatever they want, whenever they want it. "I am in control. I can get everything I want from my parents. I don't have to listen to anybody. Good things can be obtained by demanding them or by making a scene." This message eventually becomes the child's way of relating to the world in general and to other people in particular. This sets the stage for a lifetime of immaturity and a good deal of difficulty on the job and in personal relationships.

It's all right to provide for our children, but they don't need everything they want. And there is a point at which material things become liabilities rather than assets. Do your children have more toys than they can play with? Does your teenager have more money than he or she can spend? Do your kids feel entitled to everything they have rather than thankful? Do they expect to get all the latest gizmos and gadgets, regardless of the cost? If so, they may find themselves ill-equipped to survive in the real world.

The following parable, adapted from Bruce Baldwin's *Beyond the Cornucopia Kids*, highlights this truth.

> Once upon a time, there were two beautiful Luna moths, glorious in flight as their bright green wings reflected the light of the streetlights and moon. They were delighted when their own baby caterpillar came into the world. As most parents do, they looked forward to seeing their young one turn into a beautiful adult moth just like them. Because they cared so much, they gave their child everything a young caterpillar could possibly want. And when the time came, they even helped build the protective cocoon within which the metamorphosis would take place. Then they waited with eager anticipation for a gorgeous young moth to make a grand entrance into the adult world.
>
> At last they saw the cocoon breaking away. To their shock and dismay, their young caterpillar emerged without changing

at all! The small caterpillar greeted them with an explanation: "It's too tough to be a moth these days. You have to fly on your own and find your own food. And there's no one around to take care of you. I've decided to stay just the way I am and keep you company." To the parents' distress, that is just what the apprehensive young caterpillar did.

Let's help our young ones grow and take flight. Let's not handicap them by making life too easy.

THINK IT THROUGH

1. When your children were very young, how did you try to make life easy for them?
2. When did you have to rescue your young child from a severe consequence? What happened as a result? What motivated you?
3. When you were a teenager, how did your parents discipline you? Which disciplinary methods were most effective?
4. When did you learn that your actions had consequences?
5. When, recently, have you been tempted to rescue your teenagers?
6. Instead of rescuing, how could you have used the principle of allowing them to experience the consequences of their behavior?
7. What natural consequences will you try to use in disciplining your kids?
8. In what areas of parenting will you need to use logical consequences?
9. When will you and your teenagers discuss specific logical consequences for specific behaviors?

Chapter 12

Remember: Something Is Always Better than Nothing

Who won the NBA Championship last season?
Who won the World Series?

Which team won the Super Bowl?

How about the Stanley Cup?

If you're more into the local scene, who won your high school conference championship in your favorite sport?

OK, so you're not into sports at all. Well then, who won the last election for the U.S. Senate or House of Representatives from your state or district? How about the past presidential election—who won that?

Now for the big question: In all of those championships or elections where you can name the winner, what was the score?

If you can remember the score for any of those winners, you have a remarkable memory! Actually the score is irrelevant. What matters is who won. Whether by one point, run, goal, or vote, someone wins, and that's what counts.

This principle also holds true in parenting teenagers. Some people think they have to know it all and do it all . . . just right. So they go to every seminar, read all the books, and listen to tons of tapes and programs. But for many, all this advice and information results in guilt and frustration. They wonder how they can possibly do everything that they've heard and read. Feeling overwhelmed and sensitized to their own inadequacies and failings, they almost feel like giving up, like leaving the game.

If that's where you are, how you feel, then listen carefully: Don't! Don't give up or be discouraged because you aren't the perfect parent. No one is. Only one perfect person ever lived—Jesus. All the rest of us sinners and bunglers make mistakes and fall far short of perfection. We must remember that the victory is what counts, not the score. Winning 55 to 54 or even 1 to 0 will do. Doing something is always better than doing nothing.

Of course, this doesn't mean that we should become lazy or complacent—that's the quickest way to lose. We can all be a little better than we are right now. There's always room for improvement. That's called growth.

What about Proverbs 22:6?

Some Christian parents are deeply burdened with guilt because they have children who have rejected their values or their faith. Often this is because they accept Proverbs 22:6 as an absolute promise: "Teach your children to choose the right path, and when they are older, they will remain upon it" (NLT). Did God really mean it that way?

It's helpful to remember that the book of Proverbs is a collection of "wisdom sayings," which are not to be confused with the promises of God. Proverbs are principles that are *generally true* but, specifically, were never meant to be absolute.

Take, for example, Proverbs 15:1 "A gentle answer turns away wrath, but harsh words stir up anger" (NLT). What happens when your gentle answer is met with hostility? That doesn't make the proverb any less true. Most of the time, a gentle answer *does* turn away wrath, but we have no control over the response we get.

The same holds for Proverbs 22:6. While it is true that children who have been taught to "choose the right path" are more likely to "remain on it" than those who have received no teaching at all, Proverbs also says that it's common for children to despise their parents (15:20) and mock them (30:17). Indeed, children raised in a godly home may even be so heartless as to run through their parents' money! (28:24). Proverbs presents a very realistic view of life, not a storybook ideal.

If we follow the advice of Proverbs 22:6, there is a good probability that our children will either remain true to what they have been taught or return to it after they have matured. That, however, is only a probability; it is not a promise. This verse emphasizes what parents should do. That is all we have control over. If we have done the best we can to instill our faith and values in our children, then we have done our best before God. The rest is up to the children themselves and up to God. Regardless of how our kids turn out, we shouldn't take more credit than we deserve—good or bad.

But remember this—God isn't finished with our kids yet. He's not even finished with *us!*

Ask these questions: Where do I need to get better? Where do I need to grow? What is one thing I can do today to start myself on a journey of growth? It may not be very big. It could be as simple as deciding to smile the next time your teenagers walk through the door rather than greeting them with that perpetual look of frustration. Maybe it's deciding to wait a few minutes before automatically saying no. Perhaps it's planning a father-son camping trip this year as a way to do a little "male bonding." Maybe it's a commitment to knock off work a half-hour earlier this year in order to spend more time with the family.

The point is simply this: Whatever you do will make a difference. The danger is in not making any changes at all.

We don't have to do everything mentioned in this book (or any other book), but for goodness' sake, we should do something . . . because something is always better than nothing. And whatever we do, God will bless it if we will allow him to. God has a way of taking small things and turning them into big things. Just as Jesus took a little boy's lunch beside the Sea of Galilee and fed a multitude with it, so he takes the little actions, the small attempts to do what is right, and blesses them and uses them to make an incredible difference in the lives of our kids—and in our lives.

KEEP THE NEST STRONG

Everyone knows that parenting teens can be a real challenge. When kids begin the process of leaving the nest, they start spreading their wings and shaking the tree. That's why it's important to make sure that they have a strong nest to leave. One of the best gifts we can give our kids during their teen years is a secure and stable home. When teens start shaking the tree, they need a nest that won't fall. Sometimes we hear about families who literally fell apart when the children became teenagers. In most cases, it wasn't the teenagers' fault. Because the nest was already in disrepair, the first storm that came along destroyed it.

Prescribing how to build a healthy home is beyond the scope of this book, but as we come to the end of it, we would like to offer a few words of wisdom that will help to keep the nest strong and able to withstand any tree shaking that may occur during the teenage years.

Make the Main Thing the Main Thing

For Christians, the Main Thing is a personal relationship with God. Jesus said that the first and greatest commandment is to "love the Lord your God with all your heart, all your soul, all your mind, and all your strength" (Mark 12:30 NLT). Obviously, then, a relationship with God must be given the highest priority.

Some people confuse this with "doing" for God: serving him, obeying him, working hard for him. But a man doesn't love his wife best by working for her. He loves her best by being with her. Listening to her. Respecting her. Adoring her.

Henri Nouwen asked Mother Teresa the secret to human happiness. Her answer: "Spend an hour a day with God and you'll be all right." One of the very real hazards of being a parent is that we get so busy raising kids that we don't spend time alone with God—to deepen our relationship, our intimacy with him. But if we will do this consistently, we will find a spiritual center that will give us direction and purpose in life, and we will leave an indelible impression on our children.

Take Care of Yourself

Pastor Myron Augsburger is credited with saying, "You must be first a person, then a partner, then a parent, and, last of all, a professional—whatever your profession might be: plumber, painter, politician, or preacher."

Some parents spend so much time on the task of parenting that they neglect their own well-being. This does not mean that we should become self-centered. But we should realize that parents who don't take care of themselves physically and emotionally are rarely able to provide proper love and attention to their families.

We also need to work at enjoying life, at being happy—if we are unhappy, those close to us will also be unhappy. The home will take on a sort of malaise or gloom.

Here are a few tips on how to be happy (or at least a little happier):

- Try to find joy in work. Nothing makes a person unhappier than to feel stuck in a distasteful job.
- Find enjoyable hobbies and recreational activities *and do them regularly.*
- Develop meaningful friendships outside the home.
- Stay out of debt; spend less than your income.
- Stay physically healthy. Eat the right kinds of foods, exercise regularly—stay in shape.
- Keep growing and learning, or, as Steven Covey puts it, "Sharpen the Saw."

Taking care of ourselves involves having a positive attitude and having fun in life.

Love Your Spouse More than Your Kids

In two-parent homes, children need the security of knowing that their parents are totally committed to each other and that nothing a child does can alter their relationship. Moms and dads who focus more on the husband-wife relationship than they do on their kids operate from a position of great strength. A strong marriage is the best predictor of whether kids will grow up with healthy values and a positive view of the family unit.

> The greatest gift parents can give their children is their love for each other. Through that love they create an anxiety-free place for their children to grow, encouraging them to develop confidence in themselves and find the freedom to choose their own ways in life.
>
> Henri Nouwen, *Bread for the Journey* (New York: HarperCollins, 1997).

Some parents say, "We put our children first." This sounds noble, but it's actually a prescription for serious trouble. According to John Rosemond:

> By putting children first in your family, you guarantee they will become manipulative, demanding, and unappreciative of anything and everything you do for them. You guarantee they will grow up believing they can do as they please, that it's unfair of you to expect them to lift a finger of responsibility around the home, and that it's your duty to give them everything they want and serve them in every conceivable way. Putting children first in the family further guarantees that you will experience parenthood as one of the most frustrating and unrewarding things you've ever done. It further guarantees the ultimate unhappiness of your children.[1]

Really love your husband or wife. Keep that relationship strong.

Don't Try to Force Your Kids to Be You

It's easy to be disappointed because our teenagers aren't making the same "intelligent" decisions that we would make or following along our footsteps. God created each person to be unique. We have no control over how God has designed our kids. We can and should do much to give our children the best chance at success in the world, but at some point that stops and each child's own personality, talents, gifts, dreams, and desires take over.

Most older parents will admit that they have been surprised by how their kids turned out. Usually this surprise is pleasant as parents discover that their "irresponsible" teens actually figured out how to support themselves and live on their own. At times, however, the surprise is not so positive and may come with disappointment and pain. Sometimes children from "good" families decide to reject their parents' values or make decisions that harm themselves and others. Even the best parents can experience this.

It doesn't help to feel guilty when our kids are not responding as we think they should. When God made Adam and Eve, he allowed them the freedom to fail, and they did. This did not make God a poor parent. Good parents don't always have good children, and vice versa. We need to hang in there and do what's right, regardless of the outcome. Parenting comes with no guarantees.

Love Your Kids, No Matter What

Regardless of what we experience with our kids, we should never stop loving them. Teenagers will often boast about the fights they had with their parents, but they won't ever brag to another, "My parents don't love me."

Unconditional love is a lifeline to teenagers when they are

going through difficult times or periods of self-doubt. Parental love is a source of hope and comfort, even in the midst of conflict and pain. We should never use love as a weapon or a bargaining chip.

Parent's Prayer

Heavenly Father, make me a better parent. Grant me the wisdom to respond to my children with love and respect and the courage to act on it. Teach me to understand my kids better, to listen to them patiently, and to answer all their questions with honesty and gentleness.

Forbid that I should ever laugh at their mistakes, or resort to shame and ridicule when they do something that displeases me. May I never punish them for my own selfish satisfaction or just to show off my power and authority.

Let me not tempt my child to selfishness or disobedience by my example. And guide me hour by hour that I may demonstrate by all I say and do that integrity produces happiness.

Reduce the meanness in me. Help me, Lord, to hold my tongue when I am tempted to lash out in anger or frustration.

Let me not rob my kids of the opportunity to wait on themselves, to make decisions, and to learn from their mistakes.

Bless me with the bigness to grant them all their reasonable requests and the courage to deny them privileges that I know will do them harm.

Make me fair and just and kind. And fit me, O Lord, to be loved and respected and imitated by my children.

Amen.

Be Patient and Forgiving

Growing up takes time. And today, it takes even longer than it used to. During the next stretch of rough water, we should remember, "This too shall pass." The river is a long one, and smooth (or at least *smoother*) water lies ahead. Our kids are in process—God is not finished with them yet. In fact, soon we will look back on the teenage years and wonder what all the fuss was about. Believe it or not, most parents even miss the noise and chaos of having teenagers around.

We need to get used to the fact that our teenagers will disappoint us many times. They will make lots of mistakes and many poor choices. Not only do we need to be patient, but we also need to polish our forgiveness skills because our kids are going to need them. Surprisingly, teenagers forgive quite easily. They live pretty much in the moment and don't have time to worry about what happened yesterday, so they are usually more than willing to forget and move on. Parents have a more difficult time doing this. We hold grudges. We may still be angry for something the kid did three weeks (or three months!) ago. So we hold it against them and demand our pound of flesh.

This is not a good way to model the forgiveness of God, however. If we have given ourselves to God by faith, he forgives us, even for those sins we don't realize we've committed (1 John 1:9). We can do nothing to earn God's forgiveness. That's called grace, and we need to be parents who are full of grace. So we should deal with problems when they come up, then forgive and move on.

Lighten Up

Laughter is said to be the best medicine. This is especially true with teenagers in the home. Even in parenting's darkest times we need to remember that it's not all that bad. Mark

Twain once said, "My mother had a great deal of trouble with me when I was a youngster, but I think she enjoyed it." We should enjoy our kids despite the problems we have with them. That's possible—it's just a matter of perspective.

David Elkind has observed that all the healthy families he knew had one characteristic in common: laughter. Is there laughter in your home? Granted, this could be a chicken-egg situation (what came first, the laughter or the healthy home?), but there's no reason to leave it to chance. We can provide more laughter. Adolescence is not terminal, nor is it a crime. We need to lighten up!

Today Is a Good Day to Laugh

Don't you realize that when your child is nine years old, he or she is "half done"? The journey of full-time parenting is not going to last forever, so *find joy in the journey!* The message on my answering machine is the theme-song of my life: *"Enjoy today. This is not a dress rehearsal!"*

—Kendra Smiley

Be Confident

Modern parents become immobilized at times because they feel inadequate. We may think that it takes an expert (if not a village) to raise children, but if God had wanted experts, he would never have given our children to us.

Parenting isn't rocket science. While it's certainly more important than rocket science, it requires no formal education other than a willingness to learn on the job. Attending a few years of college or acquiring an advanced degree doesn't automatically make a person wise.

We know what we need to know to be good parents. We shouldn't be intimidated by all the experts or books on parenting. We can learn much from the many outstanding authors, speakers, educators, pastors, and psychologists who teach on this topic, but we shouldn't wait around for someone to tell us what to do. Those experts are not responsible for our kids. Instead, let's draw upon the resources that we do have, ask God for wisdom and guidance, and then use our best judgment.

This little poem comes from John Maxwell:

Junior hit the meter man; Junior hit the cook.
Junior's "antisocial" (according to the book).
Junior smashed the clock and lamp; Junior hacked a tree.
(Destructive trends are treated in chapters two and three.)
Junior threw his milk at mom; Junior screamed for more.
(Notes on self-assertiveness are found in chapter four.)
Junior tossed his shoes and socks out into the rain.
("Acting out" is normal; disregard the strain.)
Junior set Dad's shirt on fire; upset Grandpa's plate.
(That's to get attention; see page 38.)
Grandpa seized a slipper and turned Junior cross his knee.
(He's read nothing but the Bible since 1923.)[2]

We already have what we need.

Get Help

Almost all of the problems that parents face during their children's teen years are typical and have been dealt with by countless other parents. We can rest assured that we are not alone. If problems assault us, we have plenty of company. Many parents have a hard time understanding this fact.

If you or your teenager is struggling with something that you really feel unprepared to handle, get help. Parenting was never meant to be done alone. When serious problems occur, don't feel so embarrassed or humiliated that you don't seek wisdom and guidance from others who aren't so close to the situation. Another person's point of view or the intervention of an outside professional counselor may mean the difference between life and death.

Seek help if you or your teenager faces any of the following problems:

- substance abuse (drugs or alcohol)
- pregnancy; sexual promiscuity
- gang membership
- use of guns or other lethal weapons
- the occult
- continual depression; low self-esteem
- threats of suicide or self-mutilation
- trouble with the law (vandalism, shoplifting, burglary)
- serious decline in school performance; truancy
- signs of anorexia nervosa or bulimia; serious weight loss

This is not a comprehensive list by any means. If you are having any problems that you seem incapable of solving, get help. You need the kind of support that other family members, friends, parents, and the church can provide. Consider meeting with other parents of teenagers from time to time, just to discuss common problems and to pray for one another. Make a list of professional family counselors, organizations like "Tough

Love," and other resources in your community. You may never need to seek professional help, but in the event that you do, it's best to know in advance whom to call.

A Parent's Guide to Professional Help

When is professional help needed? Nailing down what is normal in adolescence is like trying to nail gelatin to the wall. In general, the shift from "normal" to "abnormal" occurs when teens' behavior begins to interfere with their ability to carry out daily routines or sustain relationships.

The following questions may help you decide whether your teenager is going through a harmless phase or is suffering from a serious problem. If you answer yes to any of these questions, your child needs assessment and professional help as soon as possible.

- Is your teen silent for long periods and often withdrawn socially, having few friends?
- Is your teen considering dropping out or in danger of not completing high school? Failing classes?
- Is your teen obsessed with exercise and diet? Does your teen have an eating disorder?
- Does your teen practice any form of self-mutilation in the form of teeth marks, cuts, or burns? Does he or she wear homemade tattoos?
- Is your teen involved in any kind of illegal activity? Has he or she been arrested or in trouble with the law?
- Does your teen show an excessive fear of a particular family member, other relative, or family friend? Could he or she have been sexually abused and fears to talk about it?

- Does your teen have long periods of feeling worthless, helpless, guilty, or lethargic? Does he or she suffer from depression?
- Is your home life in chaos because of your teen? Is your well-being or performance at work suffering because of your teen's problems?
- Does your teen show a strong interest in the occult? Does he or she read about black magic or involved in anti-religious activities?
- Does your teen blow up with anger and get into fights a great deal? Has he or she been involved in vandalism? Is he or she a threat to someone's physical well-being?
- Are you concerned that your teen may be sexually promiscuous? Is he or she risking venereal disease or pregnancy?
- Does your teen report hearing voices that others do not hear? Does he or she hallucinate or is out of touch with reality?
- Is your teen having serious problems with sleep, such as insomnia, repeated wakefulness at night, frequent nightmares, or sleeping too much?
- Does your teen have morbid thoughts, talk about death a lot? Is he or she suicidal?
- Does your teen run with a peer group that violates the rights of others? Do you have reason to suspect that he or she is involved in illegal activities or destructive acts?
- Does your teen get drunk? Does he or she drive while drinking? Is your teen experimenting with drugs that can kill?
- Does your teen experience relatively brief periods of intense anxiety? Does he or she suffer from panic attacks?

Les Parrott III, *Helping the Struggling Adolescent* (Grand Rapids, MI: Zondervan, 1993), 41–42.

Trust God

Finally and especially, we should never forget that we can trust God with our kids. He loves our teenagers even more than we do. He created our kids and knows them by name.

God is trustworthy. Philippians 1:6 states, "And I am sure that God, who began the good work within you, will continue his work until it is finally finished on that day when Christ Jesus comes back again" (NLT). That good work was begun even before our children were born; in fact, even before the foundation of the world was laid (Eph. 1:4)! God has known our teenagers for a long time. He will finish the job; it's not up to us. God is worth trusting. He is powerful where we are powerless.

That's why it's so important to pray regularly for our kids. God listens when we pray, and he understands what we are going through. In fact, God had a teenager himself!

Luke 2 describes Jesus, the Son of God, as a twelve-year-old boy. From that point until eighteen years later, when his public ministry began, we find very little in Scripture. So we don't know much about Jesus' adolescence. But God knows all that we are going through as parents of teenagers. One of the great gifts we can give our kids that they will never forget is to pray for them every day.

So how do you feel? After telling you not to feel overwhelmed and guilty, we gave you ten more points to remember and do—how about that! Seriously, please don't forget the main thrust of this chapter, that doing *something* is better than doing nothing. The final score is inconsequential; what matters is the victory. And you can win, even if you only score once.

Hang in there and keep praying, trusting, and learning. God will work in you and in your teenager.

THINK IT THROUGH

1. In parenting, why is doing something always better than doing nothing?
2. When have you felt most like giving up in parenting your teenagers? What did you do?
3. What other resources have you recently read, seen, or heard in an effort to help you understand your teens and improve your parenting skills?
4. What two or three facts about adolescence and teenagers that you read in this book have meant the most to you? Why?
5. What two or three ideas for parenting teens have been the most relevant to you? Why?
6. What will you do to continue your education on parenting teens?
7. What two or three actions will you take to improve your relationship with your teenagers as a result of reading this book?
8. If you find yourself in need of help in a serious problem with your teens, where will you go? What resources are available in your community and church?

Appendix A: To Promote Better Understanding

H ere are twenty-four simple ideas that will help you and your teenagers stay in touch:

Tele-Communicating

Watch a TV show or movie with your teenagers and discuss it afterward.

Rock 'n' Rap

Sit down with your adolescents and listen to one of their favorite songs. Talk about why the song is a favorite. Share a song with your teenagers that was a favorite of yours when you were young.

Do Lunch

Invite your adolescents out to lunch with you. Using the time to lecture your teenagers about what they're doing wrong, however, simply defeats its purpose. Keep the discussion positive. The point of a lunch out is to cultivate a mutual friendship. The teen years are a time of laying a foundation for the future relationship between you and your then-adult children.

View a Video

Watch several rock videos with your teenagers. Rather than criticize your adolescents' taste, try to understand why they watch the videos.

Fridge Talk

Put those refrigerator magnets to good use—place on the refrigerator short articles from the newspaper, Scripture verses, interesting quotes, anything relevant to life. Allow your adolescents to do the same. This can be a fun way to exchange ideas and communicate values. Periodically discuss at the dinner table what's been posted.

Plan an Outing

Allow your adolescents to plan a family outing. Let them choose the place (within reason and your family budget). They should also be responsible for organizing the details of the trip. The family outing could be as simple as a softball game or as involved as a camping trip.

Serve

If you've never done a service project together, you should. Volunteer your family services to a charitable organization (other than your church). You could visit a rest home, help out at the food bank, visit a hospital children's ward—anything that helps others in need. This is a fantastic way to teach your children to care about others.

Drug Education

Collect pamphlets about drugs from your school counselor or local drug rehabilitation program. Sit down with your teenagers to discuss what you learned. You do need to be talking with—not *to*—your teenagers about substance abuse on a regular basis. Do something about drugs before your kids do!

Wordplay

A good way to initiate healthy, constructive discussions with your teenagers is to grab paper and pencils and sit down together. First divide your sheets into three columns. The first column should be labeled "Teen," the second "Parent," and the third "Parent-Teen Relationship." Then each of you should write down all the words you can think of that describe the teenager, you, and the relationship you share. The words can be positive or negative. Once you have completed your lists, initiate a discussion about the activity—what was learned and how to improve the relationship you have.

Family Tree

Share a victory and a defeat that your extended family has experienced. It may be the salvation of a great-grandfather or the unnecessary divorce of an aunt. Choose events that you believe will help your adolescents learn more about the family and their lives as Christians.

Music Appreciation

Ask your teenagers to invite you to a Christian rock concert. This can be a great opportunity to talk about spiritual truths in a nonthreatening, positive way. Discuss the life style of the artist and the way the people reacted at the concert. And enjoy yourself!

Out on the Town

Adolescents often perceive that adults live boring, dull lives—which many adults actually do. Break this stereotype with your adolescents by spending a night out on the town with them. Have fun together.

The Good Old Days

Dust off your high school yearbooks and share them with your adolescents. Sit down and relate some of your early experiences as you flip through the pages of your personal history.

Share a Prayer

Share a prayer request you have with your adolescents. Then ask them if there's anything they would like for you to pray for.

What's News?

Ask your teenagers for a copy of their school newspaper. Read it, choose an interesting article about the school or its students, and discuss it with them. Even though this activity may seem trite, it shows you care about their world.

Small Is Beautiful

Don't neglect the small things in life you can do together— baking cookies, shopping, working on the car—anything that interests your adolescents and that you can do together. There's nothing like an everyday project worked on together to nurture a close relationship.

Extracurricular

The next time you attend one of your kids' extracurricular activities like a play, a ball game, or even a party, watch how the other young people act, dress, talk, and so on. Make your observations without criticizing; try instead to understand why they are doing what they are doing.

Paper-and-Pencil Fun

Have your teenagers make a list of all the things you do together. Then ask them to rank the activities from most fun to least fun. File that information for future reference and then do one of their winners together!

I Do That?

This is a fun game for your entire family—provided you're all getting along fairly well. Instruct everyone that this activity is designed not to ridicule but to open discussion about your family. Allow each family member to mimic another's good and bad habits or traits. Discuss each role-play and what family members can do to change.

Picture Autobiography

Collect pictures and other family memorabilia to create a scrapbook with your adolescents.

Sex Education

For a different way to discuss sexuality with your adolescents, flip through magazines together, looking for values about sex in ads and articles. You may be surprised at how open and honest your discussion can be. Your adolescents will inevitably get sex education from someone, whether you like it or not. Let it be from you.

What Class Was That?

An easy yet important way to demonstrate your interest in and support for your teens is to learn the names of all their teachers, as well as something about their classes. It wouldn't hurt to learn the names of your church's youth workers.

Noteworthy Activity

Get in the habit of leaving each other notes of your whereabouts. We often expect our kids to leave us notes, but we don't leave any for them in return. Writing notes to your teenagers promotes mutual trust and respect.

Read a Book

Go to a bookstore and pick up a book about today's teenagers. Then discuss some of the things you learned with your teenagers.

Appendix B: Thirty Ways to Raise Your Teenagers' Self-Esteem

A dictionary definition of *self-esteem* is "respect for or a favorable impression of oneself." That's something many teenagers today don't have—which often leads them toward self-destructive behaviors. Of course, self-esteem can't be artificially produced by motivational talks or techniques designed to pump up teens' egos. Self-esteem comes from knowing that you are valued by God and by others, that you are capable, that you are gifted, that you can contribute positively to the world, and that you can control what happens to you. These perceptions don't happen automatically but through experiences and interactions with other people, especially parents. Parents are the mirrors in which kids see themselves most clearly.

Here are thirty ways you can give your kids a favorable impression of themselves:

1. Notice when your teenagers do something right and encourage them in that behavior. Let them know that you are proud of them.
2. Make simple banners or posters telling your teenagers that you love them. Hang them up in their bedrooms.
3. The next time you want to criticize your adolescents for something, think about the following issues first:
   - Is this something they have the power to change?

- Is the criticism something they've already heard a hundred times?
- Is this a teachable moment from which they'll benefit?
- Are any of my hang-ups hidden in the criticism?

4. Try this alternative to criticism: Ask the following questions of your teenagers:
   - What did you learn from the incident?
   - What could you have done differently?
   - Is there a way I can help or support you?

5. Avoid put-downs like the plague, especially ones related to physical appearance. Making fun of cracking voices, acne, or clumsiness can be very hurtful.

6. When your teenagers want to talk, talk. Take advantage of those times. Stop whatever you're doing and give your teenagers the attention they need.

7. When you give your teenagers responsibility, let them be responsible. If you ask your son to sweep the floor and you don't like the job being done, grabbing the broom and doing it yourself doesn't teach him that he's capable. Talk him through the task or show him how—but in any case, let him do it!

8. When a choice must be made between what you want or need and what your teens want or need, *you* make the sacrifice from time to time. They will notice.

9. Love your spouse. A strong family promotes a healthy self-esteem.

10. Be specific when you assign chores and responsibilities. Don't "assume" your teenagers know what to do. Then praise them when they follow through.

11. Be reasonable with your expectations. Many times we expect far too much from our kids. The result? They give up. If your teenagers fail too often, their self-image suffers.

It's best to set positive expectations rather than high expectations.

12. Avoid comparing your children with other people's kids, or with each other. Focus on their uniqueness and help them develop their own identities.

13. Take an interest in your teenagers' friends. Learn their names.

14. Label your teenagers positively. Kids have a way of living up—or down—to the labels we hang on them.

15. Listen attentively to your teenagers. Active listening communicates respect.

16. Teach your teenagers to be problem solvers. Are you helping them learn how to solve their own problems, or do you come to the rescue? If your teens can learn to solve problems without your constant help, they'll have much greater self-esteem. Guide them, don't rescue them.

17. Let teenagers act their age. Don't rob them of their adolescence by pushing them to grow up. Many kids aren't ready to date, for example, but are pushed into it by overeager parents. Other parents push their kids to choose a career. Let teenagers grow up at their own rate.

18. Ask for forgiveness when you are wrong. What a great feeling it is for your teenagers to know you aren't perfect. It teaches them the need for forgiveness and shows them that everyone makes mistakes.

19. Model assertiveness, not aggressiveness. There's a difference. If your teenagers can learn to assert themselves without being aggressive, they'll have much higher self-images.

20. Give your teenagers the freedom to fail. Be there to support them when they fail. Help them learn to grow through failure.

21. Separate your teens from their misbehavior. You need to attack the behavior, not the person. When a father says to his son, "You're such an idiot—when will you ever get it right?" that father has focused the attention more on his son than on his son's inappropriate behavior. His son is not an idiot—but what he did was stupid.

22. Give your kids hugs. Don't be afraid to touch.

23. Respect your teenagers' privacy. Snooping without an absolutely legitimate reason is a no-no. It's tempting to eavesdrop on phone conversations or read diaries, but that doesn't build up their trust in you or good feeling in themselves.

24. Spend quality and quantity time with your teenagers. Don't have your teenagers stay home in the evenings to be with the family and then not do anything together. Have some fun!

25. Respect your children's feelings. Your teenagers need to be able to express feelings without feeling embarrassed or put down. Jesus always allowed people to express their feelings— even anger. And he often identified with those feelings.

26. Take an interest in your teenagers' interests. Show you care by attending activities they're involved in, or ask about their hobbies. Become involved with something they're involved in.

27. Set clearly defined rules and limits. If you want to frustrate your teenagers, keep the rules fuzzy. Nothing is more exasperating for them than to break a rule that they didn't know existed. Your teenagers need to know what is expected. If you are going to hold your kids accountable for their actions, you must be accountable in setting clearly defined limits. When rules are fuzzy and unclear, kids start to think, *I can't do anything right.*

28. Help your teenagers find their own niches. What do they like to do? What are they good at? Encourage your teens to follow their hearts and use the gifts and talents that God blessed them with. Don't worry that your kids seem to be wasting time with unproductive activities. Remember those pilots in the Gulf War? They developed their skills playing video games!

29. If you are concerned about your teens' self-esteem, take the initiative to have a talk. But don't be surprised if your teens aren't nearly as concerned as you are.

30. Make up one of your own: _____
    _____
    _____

Appendix C: Drugs and Alcohol: Twenty Questions for Parents

Y ou may suspect that your children or teenagers are having trouble with alcohol and other drugs, but short of smelling liquor on their breath or discovering pills in their pockets, how do you tell? While symptoms vary, there are some common tip-offs. Your answers to the following questions will help you determine if a problem exists.

1. Has your youngster's personality changed dramatically? Does he or she seem giddy, depressed, extremely irritable, hostile without reason? Do his or her moods change suddenly, intensely, and without provocation?

2. If you have liquor in the house, is it diminishing—or are other drugs of yours disappearing? (Unless you keep a close inventory, you may not detect disappearing drugs in the house for months.)

3. Has your teenager lost interest in school? In extracurricular activities, especially sports? Are grades dropping? Has a teacher complained that your youngster is sleeping or inattentive in class? Is your youngster skipping school? (Problems at school are common warning signs.)

4. Has your youngster changed friends and started hanging out with a drinking and drug-taking group? Are there weekend-long parties? (A youngster having problems with alcohol or other drugs will abandon old friends and seek those with similar attitudes and behavior.)

5. Are you missing money or objects that are easily converted into cash? (A young abuser's need for alcohol and other drugs gradually increases and becomes more expensive. The need for drugs eventually overcomes any guilt about stealing from family members or others.)

6. Have neighbors, friends, or others talked to you about your youngster's behavior or drug taking? (These reports may have substance.)

7. Has your youngster been arrested for drunkenness? Driving under the influence of alcohol or other drugs? Disorderly conduct? Delinquent acts? (Encounters with the law often indicate underlying problems with alcohol or other drugs. There is a strong correlation between delinquency and abuse of alcohol or other drugs.)

8. Does your youngster strongly defend his or her right to use alcohol or other drugs? (People defend that which is most important to them.)

9. Does your youngster "turn off" to talks about alcohol and other drug addictions? (Abusers would rather not hear anything that might interfere with their behavior, while nonabusers will listen without becoming defensive.)

10. Does your youngster get into fights with other youth? With other family members? (More than 70 percent of all beatings, stabbings, and assaults occur when one or both participants have been drinking or abusing other drugs.)

11. Are there medical or emotional problems? (Check for ulcers, bronchitis, high blood pressure, acute indigestion, liver and kidney ailments, hepatitis, diabetes, nose bleeds, malnutrition, weight loss, depression, memory lapses, and talk of suicide. Alcohol and other drugs take their toll. Youngsters on "uppers" or "downers" usually lose their appetites. The taking of PCP—"angel dust"—leads to

paranoia and hallucinations. Long-term marijuana users often develop bronchitis. Heavy drinkers experience problems with digestion, malnutrition, and depression.)

12. Do you detect physical signs—alcohol on the breath, change in pupil size in the eyes, hyperactivity, sluggishness, slurred or incoherent speech? (These are all strong clues.)

13. Does your youngster often lie to you and to others? (For young abusers, lying becomes automatic. They often fib even without a reason.)

14. Does your youngster volunteer to clean up after adult cocktail parties? (Draining half-empty glasses is a cheap high.)

15. Have you found bottles or drug paraphernalia (pipes, matches, rolling papers, vials, lighters, razor blades, small plastic bags, scales, and so on) in the bedroom, garage, van? (Parents of abusers are amazed to find stashes of alcohol or drugs under mattresses, in stereo speakers, behind insulation in garages.)

16. Is your youngster irresponsible in using the family car—taking it without permission, making excuses for not getting it home on time? (Many teenagers drink in cars and then drive, frequently causing motor-vehicle accidents.)

17. Does your youngster stay alone in his or her bedroom most of the time, bursting forth only occasionally? Does he or she resent questions about activities and destinations? (Some secrecy, aloofness, and resentment on the part of teenagers is normal. But when carried to extremes, these may signal problems with alcohol or other drugs.)

18. Have your youngster's relationships with other family members deteriorated? Does he or she avoid family gatherings that were once enjoyed? (While this is normal behavior for most teenagers, an abuser's ability to relate to

others suffers greatly—and primary family relationships are usually affected first.)

19. Has your teenager suddenly developed a preference for long-sleeved shirts? (Drug abusers wear them to cover needle marks.)

20. Has your youngster been caught dealing drugs or giving them to friends?

If your teenagers' behavior matches any of the warning signals described in this questionnaire, it is possible that they're involved with drugs or alcohol. If you'd like help in dealing with the problem, contact a counselor, health-care professional, pastor, or youth worker.

Twenty Ways to Encourage Your Children to Use Drugs

1. Never eat together as a family.
2. Don't bother to establish any "family traditions."
3. Always talk down to your kids—after all, they're just kids.
4. Punish your child in public, and never praise or reinforce positive behavior.
5. Always solve their problems and make their decisions for them.
6. Leave the responsibility for teaching morality and spiritual things to the schools and church.
7. Never let your children experience cold, fatigue, adventure, injury, risk, challenge, experimentation, failure, frustration, discouragement, or other scary stuff.
8. Threaten your children with, "If you ever try drugs, you may as well not come home."

9. Expect your children to get A's in school in all subjects.

10. Always pick up after your kids, and don't encourage them to accept responsibility.

11. Discourage your children from talking about their feelings (anger, sadness, fear, and so on).

12. Be overprotective. Don't teach your child the meaning of the word *consequence.*

13. Make your children feel that their mistakes are sins.

14. Put your children off when they ask, "Why?" by telling them, "Because I said so."

15. Lead your children to believe that you are perfect and infallible.

16. Keep your home atmosphere in a state of chaos.

17. Never tell them how much you love them; never discuss your feelings with them.

18. Never hug them or display affection for another in front of them.

19. Always expect the worst, and never give them the benefit of the doubt.

20. Never trust them.

Appendix D: Help from God's Word

The Bible has much to say to us about parenting and family life. Listed below are some pertinent Scriptures for you to read and study with your family.

ANGER

"A fool shows his annoyance at once, but a prudent man overlooks an insult" (Prov. 12:16).

"A gentle answer turns away wrath, but a harsh word stirs up anger" (Prov. 15:1).

"Better a patient man than a warrior, a man who controls his temper than one who takes a city" (Prov. 16:32).

"An angry man stirs up dissension, and a hot-tempered one commits many sins" (Prov. 29:22).

"Do not be quickly provoked in your spirit, for anger resides in the lap of fools" (Eccl. 7:9).

"'In your anger do not sin': Do not let the sun go down while you are still angry" (Eph. 4:26).

APOLOGY

"He who conceals his sins does not prosper, but whoever confesses and renounces them finds mercy" (Prov. 28:13).

"Therefore confess your sins to each other and pray for each other so that you may be healed" (James 5:16).

ARGUING

"How good and pleasant it is when brothers live together in unity!" (Ps. 133:1).

"It is to a man's honor to avoid strife, but every fool is quick to quarrel" (Prov. 20:3).

"Get rid of all bitterness, rage and anger, brawling and slander, along with every form of malice. Be kind and compassionate to one another, forgiving each other, just as in Christ God forgave you" (Eph. 4:31–32).

DISCIPLINE

"A fool spurns his father's discipline, but whoever heeds correction shows prudence" (Prov. 15:5).

"Discipline your son, and he will give you peace; he will bring delight to your soul" (Prov. 29:17).

"Moreover, we have all had human fathers who disciplined us and we respected them for it. How much more should we submit to the Father of our spirits and live! Our fathers disciplined us for a little while as they thought best; but God disciplines us for our good, that we may share in his holiness. No discipline seems pleasant at the time, but painful. Later on, however, it produces a harvest of righteousness and peace for those who have been trained by it" (Heb. 12:9–11).

DISCOURAGEMENT

"Wait for the LORD; be strong and take heart and wait for the LORD" (Ps. 27:14).

"Come to me, all you who are weary and burdened, and I will give you rest. Take my yoke upon you and learn from me, for I am gentle and humble in heart, and you will find rest for your souls. For my yoke is easy and my burden is light" (Matt. 11:28–30).

"I can do everything through him who gives me strength" (Phil. 4:13).

ENCOURAGEMENT

"Carry each other's burdens, and in this way you will fulfill the law of Christ" (Gal. 6:2).

"And we urge you, brothers, warn those who are idle, encourage the timid, help the weak, be patient with everyone" (1 Thess. 5:14).

FORGIVENESS

"If your enemy is hungry, give him food to eat; if he is thirsty, give him water to drink. In doing this, you will heap burning coals on his head, and the LORD will reward you" (Prov. 25:21–22).

"Blessed are the merciful, for they will be shown mercy" (Matt. 5:7).

"Then Peter came to Jesus and asked, 'Lord, how many times shall I forgive my brother when he sins against me? Up to seven times?' Jesus answered, 'I tell you, not seven times, but seventy-seven times'" (Matt. 18:21–22).

"Be kind and compassionate to one another, forgiving each other, just as in Christ God forgave you" (Eph. 4:32).

"Bear with each other and forgive whatever grievances you may have against one another. Forgive as the Lord forgave you" (Col. 3:13).

GUILT

"I have swept away your offenses like a cloud, your sins like the morning mist. Return to me, for I have redeemed you" (Isa. 44:22).

"So if the Son sets you free, you will be free indeed" (John 8:36).

"If we confess our sins, he is faithful and just and will forgive us our sins and purify us from all unrighteousness" (1 John 1:9).

INSTRUCTION

"Love the Lord your God with all your heart and with all your soul and with all your strength. These commandments that I give you today are to be upon your hearts. Impress them on your children. Talk about them when you sit at home and when you walk along the road, when you lie down and when you get up" (Deut. 6:5–7).

"Train a child in the way he should go, and when he is old he will not turn from it" (Prov. 22:6).

"Tell it to your children, and let your children tell it to their children, and their children to the next generation" (Joel 1:3).

LISTENING

"My dear brothers, take note of this: Everyone should be quick to listen, slow to speak and slow to become angry" (James 1:19).

LOVE

"Love is patient, love is kind. It does not envy, it does not boast, it is not proud. It is not rude, it is not self-seeking, it is not easily angered, it keeps no record of wrongs. Love does not delight in evil but rejoices with the truth. It always protects, always trusts, always hopes, always perseveres" (1 Cor. 13:4–7).

"We love because he first loved us. If anyone says, 'I love God,' yet hates his brother, he is a liar. For anyone who does not love his brother, whom he has seen, cannot love God, whom he has not seen. And he has given us this command: Whoever loves God must also love his brother" (1 John 4:19–21).

NAGGING

"When words are many, sin is not absent, but he who holds his tongue is wise" (Prov. 10:19).

"The tongue that brings healing is a tree of life" (Prov. 15:4).

"He who covers over an offense promotes love, but whoever repeats the matter separates close friends" (Prov. 17:9).

PARENT-TEEN RELATIONSHIP

"Then he [Jesus] went down to Nazareth with them [his parents] and was obedient to them. . . . And Jesus grew in wisdom and stature, and in favor with God and men" (Luke 2:51–52).

"Children, obey your parents in the Lord, for this is right. 'Honor your father and mother'—which is the first commandment with a promise—'that it may go well with you and that you may enjoy long life on the earth.' Fathers, do not exasperate your children; instead, bring them up in the training and instruction of the Lord" (Eph. 6:1–4).

"Children, obey your parents in everything, for this pleases the Lord. Fathers, do not embitter your children, or they will become discouraged" (Col. 3:20–21).

PATIENCE

"I waited patiently for the LORD; he turned to me and heard my cry" (Ps. 40:1).

"But those who hope in the LORD will renew their strength. They will soar on wings like eagles; they will run and not grow weary, they will walk and not be faint" (Isa. 40:31).

"Not only so, but we also rejoice in our sufferings, because we know that suffering produces perseverance; perseverance, character; and character, hope" (Rom. 5:3–4).

"Let us not become weary in doing good, for at the proper time we will reap a harvest if we do not give up" (Gal. 6:9).

"This calls for patient endurance on the part of the saints who obey God's commandments and remain faithful to Jesus" (Rev. 14:12).

SELF-ESTEEM

"For you created my inmost being; you knit me together in my mother's womb. I praise you because I am fearfully and wonderfully made; your works are wonderful, I know that full well" (Ps. 139:13–14).

"Therefore, if anyone is in Christ, he is a new creation; the old has gone, the new has come!" (2 Cor. 5:17).

"For we are God's workmanship, created in Christ Jesus to do good works, which God prepared in advance for us to do" (Eph. 2:10).

"For you know that it was not with perishable things such as silver or gold that you were redeemed from the empty way of life handed down to you from your forefathers, but with the precious blood of Christ, a lamb without blemish or defect" (1 Peter1:18–19).

WORRY

"Cast your cares on the Lord and he will sustain you; he will never let the righteous fall" (Ps. 55:22).

"Trust in the Lord with all your heart and lean not on your own understanding; in all your ways acknowledge him and he will make your paths straight" (Prov. 3:5–6).

"Therefore do not worry about tomorrow, for tomorrow will worry about itself. Each day has enough trouble of its own" (Matt. 6:34).

Appendix E

Memo

To: Parents

From: Your Teenager

1. Don't spoil me. I know quite well that I shouldn't get all I ask for. I'm only testing you.
2. Don't be afraid to be firm with me. I prefer it. It lets me know where I stand.
3. Don't use force with me. It teaches me that power is all that counts. I will respond better to someone who is in control.
4. Don't be inconsistent. I know you're not perfect, but when you are inconsistent in your demands or behavior, it confuses me and makes me try harder to get away with everything I can.
5. Don't make promises you can't keep. That will discourage my trust in you.
6. Don't cave in when I threaten you or say things to upset you. If you do, I'll just do it more often in order to get "victories."
7. Don't be too upset if I say things like "I hate you." I don't really mean that. I just want you to feel badly because I feel badly.
8. Don't make me feel like a child. That will only make me try to prove my adulthood in ways you probably won't like.

9. Don't do things for me that I can do for myself. It makes me feel like a child and I will never learn to take care of myself. I'll just depend on you all my life.

10. Don't let my "bad habits" get all your attention. That only encourages me to do them more.

11. Don't correct me in front of other people. I'll take more notice if you talk quietly with me in private.

12. Don't try to discuss my behavior in the heat of conflict. For some reason, my hearing is not very good at this time and my cooperation is even worse. I'll be much more open to your correction when things cool off.

13. Don't protect me from consequences. I need to learn from my experiences.

14. Don't suggest that you know everything. It gives me too much to live up to.

15. Don't scold me for my "bad attitude." I can't always help how I feel. Scold my bad actions, but try to understand my bad feelings.

16. Don't preach at me. If you do, I will protect myself by appearing to be deaf.

17. Don't demand explanations for everything I do. Sometimes I have no idea why I act the way I do.

18. Don't put me off when I ask honest questions. If you do, I'll just stop asking and get my information elsewhere.

19. Don't smother me. If you allow me plenty of time for myself or for my friends, I will look forward to those times you and I have together.

20. Don't forget to pray for me every day. I really need your prayers.

Oh, and don't forget that I love you a lot. Please don't ever stop loving me in return. . . .

Notes

Chapter 1

1. Quoted by Dr. Vernon Grounds in a speech to the National Youth Workers Convention, October 1981.
2. Patricia Hersch, *A Tribe Apart: A Journey into the Heart of American Adolescence* (New York: Fawcett-Columbine, 1998), 20.
3. William Mahedy and Janet Bernardi, *A Generation Alone* (Downers Grove, IL: InterVarsity Press, 1994), 14.
4. Edward A. Wynne and Thomas Einstein, *Chicago Tribune* (28 March 1995); quoted in *Youthworker Update* (June 1995), 8.
5. David Elkind, *Ties That Stress* (Cambridge, MA: Harvard University Press, 1994), 133.
6. USA Network in *TV Guide;* quoted in *Media Update,* vol. 3, p. 1.
7. Alvin Toffler, *Future Shock* (New York: Random House, 1970), 350–58.

Chapter 2

1. From an address presented at the National Youth Workers Convention, 1985.

Chapter 5

1. Susan Littwin, *The Postponed Generation: Why American Youth Are Growing Up Later* (New York: Morrow, 1986), 44–45.

Chapter 6

1. *Wall Street Journal*, 10 September 1997, B9.
2. "Teens and Self-Image," *USA Weekend* magazine, 1–3 May 1998, 18.
3. From an address presented at the National Youth Workers Convention, 1985.

Chapter 9

1. Erma Bombeck, Field Enterprises, Inc., 1984.
2. James Dobson, *Parenting Isn't for Cowards* (Dallas, TX: Word, 1987), 155.

Chapter 10

1. "Children Who Use Gateway Drugs Are at Greater Risk of Using Other Drugs," *The National Center on Addiction and Substance Abuse at Columbia University* (11 Dec. 1997). Quoted in Walt Mueller, *Understanding Today's Youth Culture* (Wheaton, IL: Tyndale, 1999), 300.
2. "Monitoring the Future Study: Trends in Lifetime Prevalence of Use of Various Drugs for Eighth, Tenth, and Twelfth Graders," quoted in Mueller, *Understanding Today's Youth Culture*, 304.
3. "SIECUS Fact Sheet: Adolescence and Abstinence," *SIECUS* (22 Oct. 1997), quoted in Mueller, *Understanding Today's Youth Culture*, 245.
4. Mueller, *Understanding Today's Youth Culture*, 246–48.
5. *Wall Street Journal*, 10 September 1997, B9.

Chapter 12

1. John Rosemond, *John Rosemond's Six-Point Plan for Raising Happy, Healthy Children* (Kansas City, MO: Andrews and McMeel, 1989), 7.

2. John Maxwell, *Breakthrough Parenting* (Colorado Springs, CO: Focus on the Family, 1996), 81.

Additional Resources

Aycock, Chuck, and Dave Veerman. *From Dad with Love.* Wheaton, IL: Tyndale, 1994.

Baldwin, Bruce. *Beyond the Cornucopia Kids: How to Raise Healthy, Achieving Children.* Wilmington, NC: Direction Dynamics, 1988.

Dobson, James. *Parenting Isn't for Cowards.* Dallas, TX: Word, 1987.

Elkind, David. *All Grown Up and No Place to Go: Teenagers in Crisis.* Reading, MA: Addison-Wesley, 1984.

———. *Ties That Stress.* Cambridge, MA: Harvard University Press, 1994.

Glenn, H. Stephen, and Jane Nelson. *Raising Self-Reliant Children in a Self-Indulgent World.* Rocklin, CA: Prima Publishing, 1989.

Habermas, Ronald T. *Raising Teens While They're Still in Preschool.* Joplin, MO: College Press, 1998.

Habermas, Ronald T., and David Olshine. *How to Have a Real Conversation with Your Teen.* Cincinnati, OH: Standard Publishing, 1998.

Hersch, Patricia. *A Tribe Apart: A Journey into the Heart of American Adolescence.* New York: Fawcett-Columbine, 1998.

Huggins, Kevin. *Parenting Adolescents.* Colorado Springs, CO: NavPress, 1993.

Kesler, Jay. *Raising Emotionally Healthy Teenagers.* Nashville, TN: Word, 1998.

Langston, Teresa A. *Parenting without Pressure.* Colorado Springs, CO: Pinion Press, 1994.

Males, Mike A. *The Scapegoat Generation: America's War on Adolescents.* Monroe, ME: Common Courage Press, 1996.

Maxwell, John. *Breakthrough Parenting.* Colorado Springs, CO: Focus on the Family, 1996.

Mueller, Walt. *Understanding Today's Youth Culture.* Wheaton, IL: Tyndale, 1999.

Nelson, Jane, and Lynn Lott. *Positive Discipline for Teenagers.* Rocklin, CA: Prima Publishing, 1994.

Olshine, David, and Ron Habermas. *Down But Not Out Parenting: 50 Ways to Win with Your Teen.* Cincinnati, OH: Standard Publishing, 1995.

Parrott, Les, III. *Helping the Struggling Adolescent.* Grand Rapids, MI: Zondervan, 1993.

Rice, Wayne. *Enjoy Your Middle Schooler.* Grand Rapids, MI: Zondervan, 1994.

———. *Junior High Ministry.* Grand Rapids, MI: Zondervan, 1999.

———, ed. *God's Word for Students.* Grand Rapids, MI: World Bible Publishers, 1996.

Rosemond, John. *John Rosemond's Six-Point Plan for Raising*

Happy, Healthy Children. Kansas City, MO: Andrews and McMeel, 1989.

Sanders, Bill. *Seize the Moment, Not Your Teen*. Wheaton, IL: Tyndale, 1997.

Veerman, Dave. *Getting Your Kid to Talk*. Wheaton, IL: Tyndale, 1994.

———. *How to Apply the Bible*. Grand Rapids, MI: Baker Book House, 1999.

———. *Ozzie & Harriet Had a Scriptwriter: Making Tough Choices with your Teens in the Real World*. Wheaton, IL: Tyndale, 1996.

———. *Parenting Passages*. Wheaton, IL: Tyndale, 1994.

———. *Reaching Kids before High School*. Wheaton, IL: Victor Books, 1995.

———, ed. *Ready for Life—40 Practical Life Skills Your Kids Will Need to Stay Afloat*. Wheaton, IL: Tyndale, 1998.

———, ed. *Student's Life Application Bible*. Wheaton, IL: Tyndale, 1997.

Why Not Schedule an Understanding Your Teenager Seminar at Your Church?

Wayne Rice, Dave Veerman, and the rest of the Understanding Your Teenager seminar team travel to churches all over North America every year presenting the ideas and principles found in this book. The seminar is three hours in length and can be scheduled for a weeknight or weekend day of your choice.

For information on how to bring an Understanding Your Teenager seminar to your church, write or phone:

Understanding Your Teenager
P.O. Box 420
Lakeside, CA 92040
(800) 561-9309

Or visit us on the Web: http://www.uyt.com

About the Authors

Wayne Rice is the founder and director of the Understanding Your Teenager seminars. He is a veteran youth worker and has written numerous books and articles on youth, youth ministry, and parenting. He is also the cofounder of Youth Specialties, an organization that provides resources and training for youth workers.

Dave Veerman worked with Youth for Christ for twenty-six years in Illinois and Louisiana and served as the National Director of Campus Life. He has written many books on youth ministry and parenting including *Reaching Kids before High School, From Dad with Love, Getting Your Kid to Talk,* and *Parenting Passages.* He is a partner of The Livingstone Corporation and is a member of the Understanding Your Teenager seminar team.